The Philosophy of Zen Buddhism

Byung-Chul Han

The Philosophy of Zen Buddhism

Translated by Daniel Steuer

polity

Originally published in German as *Philosophie des Zen-Buddhismus*
© Philipp Reclam jun. Verlag GmbH, Ditzingen, 2002

This English edition © Polity Press, 2022

Polity Press
65 Bridge Street
Cambridge CB2 1UR, UK

Polity Press
111 River Street
Hoboken, NJ 07030, USA

ISBN-13: 978-1-5095-4509-4
ISBN-13: 978-1-5095-4510-0 (paperback)

A catalogue record for this book is available from the British Library.

Library of Congress Control Number: 2022933624

Typeset in 10.75 on 14pt Janson Text
by Cheshire Typesetting Ltd, Cuddington, Cheshire
Printed and bound in Great Britain by TJ Books Ltd, Padstow, Cornwall

The publisher has used its best endeavours to ensure that the URLs for external websites referred to in this book are correct and active at the time of going to press. However, the publisher has no responsibility for the websites and can make no guarantee that a site will remain live or that the content is or will remain appropriate.

Every effort has been made to trace all copyright holders, but if any have been overlooked the publisher will be pleased to include any necessary credits in any subsequent reprint or edition.

For further information on Polity, visit our website:
politybooks.com

CONTENTS

PREFACE

Zen Buddhism is a form of Mahāyāna Buddhism that originated in China and is strongly focused on meditation.[1] What is peculiar to Zen Buddhism is expressed by the following verse, attributed to its founder, Bodhidharma,[2] a figure surrounded by legend:

A special tradition outside the scriptures;
No dependence upon words and letters;
Direct pointing at the soul of man;
Seeing into one's own nature,
and the attainment of
Buddhahood.[3]

This scepticism towards language and distrust of conceptual thought, so typical of Zen Buddhism, explains why Zen Buddhist sayings are so enigmatic and succinct. What is said shines because of what is not said. Zen Buddhist masters also make use of unusual forms of communication. They often respond to questions of the form 'What is . . .?' with a blow of the stick.[4] And where words do not get the point across, loud shouting might be used instead.

Despite Zen Buddhism's fundamental hostility towards theory and discourse, a philosophy of Zen Buddhism need not necessarily end up as a (paradoxical) epic of haikus, for it is possible to reflect philosophically on a subject matter that is not itself philosophy in the narrower sense. One may linguistically circle silence without thereby drowning it out with language. The present philosophy of Zen Buddhism is nourished by a *philosophizing about* and *with* Zen Buddhism. It aims conceptually to unfold the philosophical force inherent in Zen Buddhism. This undertaking is not, however, altogether without its problems. The experiences of being or of consciousness that the practice of Zen Buddhism works towards cannot fully be captured in conceptual language. *The Philosophy of Zen Buddhism* tries to turn this linguistic difficulty around by using certain linguistic strategies to convey meaning.

The present study is designed as a 'comparative' one. The philosophies of Plato, Leibniz, Fichte, Hegel, Schopenhauer, Nietzsche, Heidegger and others will be confronted with the insights of Zen Buddhism. The comparative approach is a method for disclosing meaning.

Haikus are frequently woven into the individual sections of the text. The intention behind this is not, however, to illustrate abstract matters with haikus, and still less is it to produce philosophical interpretations of haikus. The haikus and the individual sections of text relate to each other as neighbours. The quoted haikus aim to put the reader in the mood of the textual passages to which they relate. The haikus should be seen as beautiful frames that quietly talk to their pictures.[5]

A Religion without God

See the great Buddha
he is dozing and dozing
all through the spring day.
— Shiki

In his lectures on the philosophy of religion, Hegel says that the subject matter of religion is 'God and nothing but God'.[1] Buddhism being no exception, Hegel simply equates the central concept of Buddhism, 'nothing', with God:

> nothing and not-being is what is ultimate and supreme. It is nothing alone which has true independence; all other actuality, all particularity, has none at all. Out of nothingness everything has proceeded; into nothingness everything returns. Nothing, nothingness is the One, the beginning and the ending of everything. . . . That man should think of God as nothingness must at first sight seem astonishing, must appear to us a most peculiar idea. But, considered more

1

closely, this determination means that God is absolutely nothing determined. He is the Undetermined; no determinateness of any kind pertains to God; He is the Infinite. This is equivalent to saying that God is the negation of all particularity.[2]

In other words, Hegel interprets Buddhism as a kind of 'negative theology'. The 'nothing' expresses the negativity of God, the fact that He escapes any positive determination. Following this controversial account of the Buddhist concept of nothingness, Hegel voices his bewilderment: 'God, although actually conceived of as nothingness, as Essence generally, is yet known as a particular immediate human being', by which he means the Buddha. That 'a man with all his sensuous needs should be looked upon as God, as He who eternally creates, maintains, and produces the world', Hegel holds, is a 'conjunction' that 'may appear to us the most offensive, revolting, and incredible of all'.[3] The 'absolute' – and in Hegel's view this is a contradiction – 'has to be worshipped in the immediate finite nature of a human being':[4] 'A human being is worshipped, and he is as such the god who assumes individual form, and in that form gives himself up to be reverenced.'[5] Within this 'individual existence', he says, the Buddha is the 'substance' that is responsible for the 'creating and maintaining of the world, of nature, and of all things'.[6]

In his interpretation of Buddhism, Hegel makes use of ontotheological concepts such as substance, essence, God, power, domination and creation. This is problematic, as these concepts are all incompatible with Buddhism. The Buddhist 'nothing' is anything but a 'substance'. It is not 'existing in itself' [*in sich seiend*],[7] nor is it 'at rest within itself and persists'.[8] Rather, it is *empty within itself*, so to speak. It does not *flee* from being determined in order to retreat into its infinite inwardness. The Buddhist nothing is not that 'substantial

2

Power which governs the world, causes everything to origi-
nate and come into being in accordance with rational laws
of connection'.⁹ The nothing rather indicates that *nothing
rules*. It does not reveal itself to be a *master*. No 'rule' and
no 'power' emanates from it. Buddha *represents* nothing. He
does not embody an infinite substance in a separate individual
form. Hegel illegitimately entangles the Buddhist nothing
in representational and causal relations. His thought, which
focuses on 'substance' and 'subject', is not capable of grasping
the Buddhist nothing.

The following koan from the *Bi-yan-lu* would seem out-
landish to Hegel: 'A monk asked Dongshan, "What is the
Buddha?" Dongshan said, "Three pounds of flax."'¹⁰ Hegel
would be equally bewildered by the following words from
Dōgen: 'When you talk about the Buddha, you think the
Buddha must have various physical characteristics and a radiant
halo. If I say that the Buddha is broken tiles and pebbles, you
show astonishment.'¹¹ In response to these Zen sayings, Hegel
might claim that, in Zen Buddhism, God does not appear
as an individual but rather unconsciously 'staggers' through
various things. For Hegel, Zen Buddhism would therefore
constitute a regression from ordinary Buddhism, because the
latter's 'advance' over the 'fantastic' religion consists precisely
in the fact that God's 'chaotic stagger' is 'reduced to a state
of rest', that the 'arid disorder' is returned 'into itself and
into essential unity'. For Hegel, Buddhism is a 'religion of
Being-within-itself'. In such a religion, God collects Himself
into Himself. All 'relation to another is now cut off'.¹² The
fantastic religion, by contrast, does not involve this self-col-
lection. In the fantastic religion, the 'One'¹³ is not with itself;
rather, it 'staggers'. In Buddhism, however, God is no longer
dispersed into countless things: 'Thus, as compared with the
previous stage, there is an advance made here from fantastic
personification split up into a countless multitude of forms,

to a personification which is enclosed within definite bounds, and is actually present.' This God, who has collected Himself into Himself, appears 'in an individual concentration', namely in the form of a human individual who is called Buddha.[14]

Hegel's interpretation of Buddhist meditation also fails to grasp Buddhism's spiritual attitude. According to Hegel, in meditative contemplation the goal is 'the stillness of being-within-itself'.[15] In this 'being-within-itself . . . all relation to another is now precluded'.[16] Thus, in 'meditation' man 'is occupied with himself';[17] he is 'returning into himself'.[18] Hegel even talks of 'self-absorption' [*An-sich-selbst-Saugen*].[19] The aim is a pure, absolute inwardness of being-within-itself that is completely free of another. One immerses oneself in 'abstract thought in itself', which is 'active substantiality' and constitutive of the 'creation and preservation of the world'.[20] The 'holiness of a man consists in his uniting himself in this extinction, in this silence, with God, with nothingness, with the Absolute'.[21] In this state of nirvana, Hegel says, 'man is without gravity, he has no longer any weight, is not subject to disease, to old age, to death; he is looked upon as God Himself; he has become Buddha'.[22] In the state of nirvana, man reaches an infinity, an immortality, that represents infinite freedom. This freedom Hegel imagines as follows:

The thought of immortality is implied in the fact that man is a *thinking* being, that he is in his freedom at home with himself; thus he is absolutely independent; an 'Other' cannot break in upon his freedom: he relates himself to himself alone; an Other cannot assert itself within him.

This equality with myself, 'I', this self-contained existence, this true Infinite, is what, according to this point of view, is immortal, is subject to no change; it is itself the Unchangeable, what is within itself alone, what moves itself only within itself.[23]

4

Accordingly, infinity as freedom consists in a pure inwardness that is in no way entangled with anything external or other. In this immersion in pure thinking, human beings are wholly with themselves, only relate to themselves, only touch themselves. Nothing external disturbs this self-referential contemplation. In Hegel's version of Buddhism, God is characterized by this pure 'inwardness' of the 'I'. We shall see later that in fact the Buddhist nothing is opposed to inwardness.

According to Hegel, the God of all religions, and especially the God of Christianity, is not only 'substance' but also 'subject'.[24] God is to be imagined, like the human being, as a subject, a person. However, the Buddhist nothing, according to Hegel, lacks subjectivity and personality. Like the Indian God, it is not 'the One Person' but 'the One in a neuter sense'.[25] It is not yet a '*He*', not a *master*. It lacks 'exclusive subjectivity'.[26] It is not as exclusive as the Jewish God. The figure of the Buddha compensates for this lack of subjectivity. The 'absolute' is personified and 'worshipped' in an empirical, finite individual. However, as we have already seen, for Hegel the fact that a finite human being is considered to be God 'may appear to us the most offensive, revolting, and incredible of all'. For Hegel, it is a contradiction to imagine the absolute in the form of a finite individual. But Hegel's view rests on a misinterpretation of Buddhism. Hegel declares the Christian religion to be the final form of religion, and for Christianity the figure of the person is constitutive. Hegel projects Christianity onto Buddhism, and this leads him to believe that Buddhism is lacking. He thereby fails to recognize the radical alterity of Buddhist religion. The Zen master Linji's demand that one should 'kill the Buddha' would be wholly incomprehensible to Hegel: 'if you meet a buddha, kill the buddha. . . . Then for the first time you will gain emancipation, will not be entangled with things, will pass freely anywhere you wish to go.'[27]

The Buddhist nothing's lack of 'exclusive subjectivity' or 'conscious will' is not a 'deficiency' but a strength of Buddhism.[28] The absence of 'will' or 'subjectivity' is precisely what constitutes the peacefulness of Buddhism. Further, because the category of 'power' is an expression of 'substance' or 'subject', it does not apply to the Buddhist nothing. 'Power' that 'reveals' or 'manifests' *itself* is alien to the nothing, which lacks substance and subjectivity. The nothing does not represent an 'acting, effective power'; it does not 'effect' anything.[29] The absence of a 'master' further distances Buddhism from any economy of domination. Because 'power' is not concentrated in a *name*, Buddhism is non-violent. There is no individual who represents a 'power'. Buddhism's foundation is an empty centre that does not exclude anything, that is not occupied by a holder of power. This emptiness, this absence of 'exclusive subjectivity', is what makes Buddhism friendly. Its nature is incompatible with 'fundamentalism'.

Buddhism does not allow for the invocation of God. It does not know the divine inwardness into which such an invocation would delve, nor the human inwardness that would require such an invocation. It is free of the *urge to invoke*. The 'immediate impulse', 'longing' and 'instinct of spirit' that insists on God being concrete and concentrated 'in the form of a real man' (i.e. Christ) is alien to Buddhism.[30] In God in human form, the human being sees *himself*. In God, the human appreciates *himself*. Buddhism, by contrast, does not have a narcissistic structure.

The Zen master Dongshan would shatter 'God' with his 'sword that kills'.[31] Zen Buddhism leads the Buddhist religion towards strict immanence in the most radical way: 'Vast and empty. Nothing holy!'[32] The Zen sayings about Buddha being 'broken tiles and pebbles' or 'three pounds of flax' indicate the orientation towards immanence in the spiritual attitude of Zen Buddhism. They express the 'everyday mind'

6

that makes Zen Buddhism a *religion of immanence*.[33] The nothing, or emptiness, of Zen Buddhism is not directed at a divine *There*. The radical turn towards immanence, towards *Here*, is a reflection of the Chinese, or Far Eastern, character of Zen Buddhism.[34] Like Linji, the Zen master Yunmen urges the *destruction of the holy*. He seems to understand what *peace* depends upon:

> Master Yunmen related [the legend according to which] the Buddha, immediately after his birth, pointed with one hand to heaven and with the other to earth, walked a circle in seven steps, looked at the four quarters, and said, 'Above heaven and under heaven, I alone am the Honored One.'
>
> The Master said, 'Had I witnessed this at the time, I would have knocked him dead with one stroke and fed him to the dogs in order to bring about peace on earth!'[35]

The worldview of Zen Buddhism is not directed *upwards*, nor is it oriented towards a *centre*. It lacks a ruling centre. One might also say: the centre is everywhere. Every being forms a centre. As *friendly* beings that do not exclude anything, each being reflects the whole in itself. All beings de-internalize themselves, open up boundlessly towards a world-like openness: 'Someone who has come to know a single particle knows the whole universe.'[36] In a single plum blossom, the whole universe blooms.

The world that *fits* into a 'single particle' has certainly been emptied of any theological-teleological 'meaning'. It is also empty in the sense that it is occupied neither by *theos* nor by *anthropos*. It is free of the complicity between *anthropos* and *theos*. The nothing of Zen Buddhism does not offer anything to hold on to, no solid 'ground' that one could be sure of or ascertain, nothing that one could cling to. The world is without a ground: 'There is no roof over the head and no earth under the feet.'[37] 'With one blow the vast sky suddenly breaks into pieces. / Holy, worldly, both vanished without trace. In the untreadable ends the way.'[38] The spiritual force of Buddhism is that it can transform the groundless into a unique hold and abode, can enable one to *inhabit* the nothing, can turn the great doubt into a *Yes*. The path does not lead into 'transcendence'. One cannot flee from the world, because there is no other world. 'There is a turning in the untreadable and a new way, or rather the *old* one, suddenly opens out. The bright moon shines in front of the temple and there is a rustling wind.' The path ends in the *age-old*, leads to a deep immanence, to an everyday world of 'men and women, young and old, pan and kettle, cat and spoon'.[39]

Zen meditation differs radically from the Cartesian meditations, which, as is well known, are based on the aim of achieving certainty and save themselves from doubt by way of the 'I' and 'God'. Zen master Dōgen would suggest that Descartes continue with his meditations, pushing and deepening his doubt even further, to the point at which he himself becomes the great doubt in which the 'I' as well as the idea of 'God' are shattered completely. Having reached the point of that doubt, Descartes would probably have exclaimed *neque cogito neque sum*, I do not think, nor am I: 'The realm of nonthinking can hardly be fathomed by cognition; in the sphere of genuine suchness there is neither "I" nor "other."'[40]

According to Leibniz, for the existence of every individual thing there must be a ground: 'Furthermore, assuming that things must exist, we must be able to give a reason for why they must exist in this way, and not otherwise.'[41] This question of reasons necessarily leads to the ultimate reason, which is called 'God': 'And that is why the ultimate reason of things must be in a necessary substance in which the diversity of changes is only eminent, as in its source. This is what we call God.'[42] Having reached this 'ultimate reason of things', thinking, the asking for a 'why', becomes *calm*. Zen Buddhism strives for a different kind of calmness. This is reached precisely by suspending the 'why' question, the question that asks for grounds. The metaphysical God, the ultimate reason, is juxtaposed with a blossoming ground-lessness: 'Red flowers bloom in glorious profusion.'[43] The following Zen saying refers to a unique calmness: 'Yesterday, today, it is just as it is. In the sky the sun rises and the moon wanes. In front of the window, the mountain rises high and the deep river flows.'[44]

As we know, Heidegger's thinking also does without the metaphysical idea of a ground in which the 'why' question becomes calm, an explanatory ground from which the being of all beings is derived. Heidegger quotes Silesius: 'The rose is without why: it blooms because it blooms.'[45] Heidegger juxtaposes this 'without why' with the 'principle of reason': *Nihil est sine ratione* (nothing is without a ground). It is certainly not easy to linger in or to inhabit the groundless. Is it therefore necessary to invoke God? Heidegger again quotes Silesius: 'A heart that is calm in its ground, God-still, as he will, / Would gladly be touched by him: it is his lute-play.'[46] Without God, the heart would thus be without 'music'. If God does not play, the world does not sound. Does the world therefore need God? The world of Zen Buddhism is not only devoid of a 'why' but also utterly devoid of divine 'music'. If we listen more carefully to haikus, we find that even they are not 'musical'. They contain no *desire*, are free of any *invocation* or *longing*. They therefore seem *dull*.[47] This *intense* dullness is what accounts for their depth.

Rain in the winter
  A mouse runs across the strings
    Of a mandolin

              – Buson

In 'Why Poets?' Heidegger writes:

> The default of God means that a God no longer gathers men
> and things to himself visibly and unmistakably and from this
> gathering ordains world-history and man's stay within it.
> . . . With this default, the ground for the world ceases to be
> grounding. . . . Ground is the soil for taking root and stand-
> ing. The age for which the ground fails to appear hangs in
> the abyss [*Abgrund*].[48]

Heidegger's God is certainly not the metaphysical God, the
ultimate ground of all things or the *causa sui*. As we know,
Heidegger consistently distanced himself from that God

> that is the cause as *causa sui*. This is the right name for the
> god of philosophy. Man can neither pray nor sacrifice to this
> god. Before the *causa sui*, man can neither fall to his knees in
> awe nor can he play music and dance before this god.[49]

In the end, Heidegger holds on to God, so his thinking
cannot really be taken to be in the vicinity of Zen Buddhism.
Zen Buddhism does not know the divine counterpart in
the face of which one can 'pray', 'dance', 'play music' or
'fall to one's knees in awe'. The *freedom* of the 'everyday
mind' consists rather in not kneeling down in awe. Its
mental attitude is better expressed as 'sitting unmovable like
a mountain'.

In his essay '. . . Poetically Man Dwells . . .', Heidegger
writes:

> Everything that shimmers and blooms in the sky and thus
> under the sky and thus on earth, everything that sounds and
> is fragrant, rises and comes – but also everything that goes
> and stumbles, moans and falls silent, pales and darkens. Into

this ... the unknown imparts himself, in order to remain guarded within it as the unknown.[50]

Thus the unknown god appears as the unknown by way of the sky's manifestness. This appearance is the measure against which man measures himself.[51]

Zen Buddhism would not allow this strict distinction between the known and the unknown, between what is manifest and what is concealed. Everything that shimmers and blooms, that is fragrant and sounds, comes, goes and stumbles, moans and falls silent, pales and darkens between heaven and earth, would already be the *measure*. There is no searching for something hidden *behind* the phenomena. The secret is what is manifest. There is no higher plane of being that precedes what is manifest, the phenomena as they appear. The nothing inhabits the same plane of being as appearances. The world *is wholly there* in a plum blossom. There is nothing outside the manifest presence of heaven and earth, of plum blossom and moon, nothing outside the things that appear in their own light. If the monk were to have asked his master 'Is there a measure on earth?' the answer might have been 'broken tiles and pebbles'. Haikus allow the *whole* world to appear within things. The world is wholly manifest in the manifest presence of things between heaven and earth. Nothing remains 'hidden'; nothing retreats to an unknown place.

Heidegger also conceives of the thing from the perspective of the world. The essence of the thing, he thinks, consists in the way it makes the world manifest. It gathers and reflects in itself earth and heaven, deities and mortals. The thing *is* the world. But for Heidegger not all things are able to make the world manifest. Heidegger's theological compulsion, the fact that he holds on to God,[52] has a selective effect on things.

11

'God' *constricts* Heidegger's 'world'. He would, for instance, not be able to include 'vermin' in his collection of things.[53] In his thing world, there are places only for the 'bull' and the 'deer'. The world of haikus, by contrast, is also populated by numerous insects and animals that would not be fit for sacrifice. This world is fuller and more friendly than Heidegger's, because it is freed not only of the *anthropos* but also of the *theos*.

> One human being,
> one fly,
> in a large room
>   – Issa[54]

> Fleas, lice
> a horse peeing
> near my pillow
>   – Bashō[55]

In *The World as Will and Representation*, Schopenhauer writes: 'If we turn from the forms . . . and go to the root of things, we shall find generally that Sakya Muni [i.e. Buddha] and Meister Eckhart teach the same thing.'[56] Some terms of Eckhart's mysticism, such as 'nothing' or 'giving up' [*Gelassenheit*], certainly suggest such a comparison. But if we look at them more closely, if we really get to the bottom of them, we will in fact detect a fundamental difference between Eckhart's mysticism and Buddhism. It is not rare for comparisons to be drawn between the two, but the idea of God at the root of Eckhart's mysticism is utterly alien to Zen Buddhism, this religion of immanence. His mysticism takes its bearings from a transcendence that, while it may – because of its negativity, which deprives it of any positive predicate – dissolve into a 'nothing', nevertheless condenses into an extraordinary substance

12

beyond the world of predicates. As opposed to the 'nothing' of Eckhart's mysticism, the nothing of Zen Buddhism is a phenomenon belonging to immanence.

The inner life of Eckhart's God also has something narcissistic about it. 'When God made man', he writes, 'He wrought in the soul His like work'. 'Making' brings about an inner identification between the maker and what is made: 'what I make, I make myself and in myself, imprinting my image expressly in it'.[57] What is made is *my* image. I see *myself* in what I make. This reflexive structure is inherent to the relation between God and His creatures: 'God loves Himself and His nature, His being and His Godhead. In the love in which God loves Himself, He loves all creatures ... God savors Himself. In the savoring in which God savors Himself, therein He savors all creatures.'[58] This 'something in the soul' which merges with God is 'the very thing that enjoys itself, the way God enjoys himself'.[59] Enjoying *oneself*, savouring *oneself* and loving *oneself* are all forms of narcissistic inwardness. This divine autoeroticism illustrates the difference between Eckhart's mysticism and Zen Buddhism. For Eckhart, God's words 'I am that I am'[60] express the 'turned-back orientation towards and by way of oneself and a firm and solid resting-in-oneself'. The 'turned-back orientation towards and by way of oneself', this reflexive structure of God, is alien to the nothing of Zen Buddhism. The nothing does not gather or condense itself into an 'I'. The subjective inwardness that makes possible the savouring of *oneself*, the enjoying of *oneself*, is absent from the fasting heart of Zen Buddhism. The nothing of Zen Buddhism is completely emptied of *any relation to self*, of inwardness.

The inner life of Eckhart's God is determined by actionism, which finds expression in a 'giving-birth-to-oneself that glows inside, and flows and boils within and across itself, a light that wholly and thoroughly permeates itself in the light and towards the light, and that everywhere is wholly and thoroughly bent and turned back on to itself'. The divine life is an 'outpouring in which something swells within itself and initially flows into itself, each part into each part, before it boils over and pours itself into the outside'.[61] Josef Quint, the editor of Meister Eckhart's German sermons and treatises, remarks in his introduction:

> For it may seem as if this empty vessel was good for nothing but staring dully and idly into the silent desert of infinity. But no, what leaves the unmistakeable imprint of the occidental feeling about the world on Meister Eckhart's mysticism, the imprint of an infinite urge to become and to do, is the fact that for Eckhart the eternal peace in God, our Lord, cannot be thought or conceived of other than as an eternal urging and becoming. In Eckhart's vigorous thinking, the silent desert of the infinite being of divine reason is a process containing infinite energy . . . it is for him comparable to an infinite, fiery, fluid flow of ore which, boiling, continuously permeates itself with itself, before pouring itself out into creaturely being.[62]

Rudolf Otto recognizes in Eckhart's God the restless 'dynamic' of 'a mighty inward *movement*, of an eternal process of ever-flowing life': 'The Deity of Eckhart is causa sui, but this not in the merely exclusive sense, that every foreign causa is shut out, but in the most positive sense of a ceaseless self-production of Himself.'[63] There is no such incessant activity in the nothing of Zen Buddhism. The 'occidental feeling about the world' filled with an 'infinite urge to become and to do' is not the Zen Buddhist feeling about the world. Zen Buddhist practice consists, on the contrary, in liberating oneself from this 'eternal urging'. The nothing of Zen Buddhism is *empty* in the sense that it does not swell within it*self*, pour

14

itself into the outside, or boil over. It does not have the full-ness of the *self*, that full, profuse, overflowing inwardness.

Eckhart distinguishes between God and Godhead. The Godhead is older than God, so to speak, older than the latter's 'active work' and creation as *making*.[64] God 'works' [*wirkt*]. In the case of the Godhead, by contrast, 'there is nothing for it to do, there is no activity in it'.[65] The Godhead is situated outside of *actu*-ality [*Wirk-lichkeit*]. We are repeatedly asked to accept God as He is *in Himself*, that is, as Godhead. Any predicate, any property, is a 'clothing' that conceals God's being-in-itself. We should accept God 'in the pure and naked substance where He is nakedly apprehending Himself':[66] 'For goodness and justice are God's garment which covers Him. Therefore, strip God of all His clothing – seize Him naked in his robing room [*kleithûs* = clothing house], where He is uncovered and bare in Himself.'[67] God even has to be de-personalized:

> for if you love God as He is God, as He is spirit, as He is person and as He is image – all that must go! – 'Well, how should I love Him then?' – You should love Him as He is: a non-God, a non-spirit, a non-person, a non-image; rather, as He is a sheer pure limpid One, detached from all duality. And in that One may we eternally sink from something to nothingness.[68]

God is nothingness: He is 'beyond all speech'.[69] Every image 'deprives you of the whole of God'. As soon as an image enters the soul, 'God has to leave with all his Godhead'. But 'when the image goes out, God comes in'.[70] Any idea of God would only be something imagined [*Ein-bild-ung*] that has to be negated in favour of the 'pure and naked sub-stance'. The soul's landscape of images is to be destroyed. Only this destruction 'seizes Him in His desert and in His

15

proper ground'.[71] Any *imagined* closeness to God, by contrast, forces Him from the soul: 'Man's highest and dearest leave-taking is if he takes leave of God for God.'[72] Only in this state of 'leave-taking' (*gelâzenheit*)[73] does God show himself as He is 'in himself'.[74] One has to kill the imagined God, so to speak, so that God can be in Himself: 'Therefore I pray to God to make me free of God, for my essential being is above God, taking God as the origin of creatures.'[75] Becoming free of God, or taking leave of God for God – these Eckhartian formulations are, of course, reminiscent of Linji: 'if you meet a Buddha, kill the Buddha'. But this latter killing does not take place for the sake of a transcendence that shines from beyond or 'above' the killed image. Rather, it makes immanence shine.

According to Eckhart, any intentional striving for God will miss the Godhead. If the fundamental trait [*Grundzug*] of the soul were the will, then it would have to *go under and sink to the ground* [*zu Grunde gehen*]. Only at the 'ground of the soul', where the soul is dead to *itself*, *is* there God.[76] 'Self-abandonment' [*Gelassenheit*] would be nothing other than this going under and sinking to the *ground* of the soul [Zu-*Grunde*-Gehen].[77] Dying means living in 'poverty', without any desire to know or to possess, that is, being there without taking pleasure *in one's own* knowledge and possession:

> I declare, that a man should be so acquitted and free that he neither knows nor realizes that God is at work in him: in that way can a man possess poverty. . . . To be poor in spirit, a man must be poor of all his own knowledge: not knowing any *thing*, not God, nor creature nor himself.[78]

Gelâzenheit means non-willing. One must not even will the non-willing. However, *gelâzenheit* does not transcend the dimension of the will altogether, because it involves the

16

human being letting go of his own will in favour of the will of God, this 'dearest will'.[79] Although one must not will to correspond to the will of God, the will of human beings is *preserved* in God. It *goes under and sinks to the ground* [*richtet sich zu Grunde*] in the sense that it *preserves itself* in that ground that, in turn, expresses itself as a will. The nothing of Zen Buddhism, by contrast, leaves the dimension of the will as such.

Eckhart holds on to the metaphysical distinction between essence and accident [*mitewesen*].[80] Human beings should meet God in His 'pure and naked substance', without any 'clothing' on him. The nothing of Zen Buddhism, by contrast, stands in opposition to substance. It is stripped not only of the 'clothing' but also of the 'wearer' of the clothing. It is *empty*. There is *no one* to be found in the 'robing room'. The emptiness is therefore not a 'nakedness'. Zen Buddhism allows what is said to shine only in what is not said, but this silence does not favour an inexpressible 'being' that is 'above' what can be said. The shining does not descend from above. Rather, it is the brilliance of things as they appear, that is, the brilliance of immanence.

At the deepest level, the desire for complete union with God exhibits a narcissistic structure. In the *unio mystica*, a human being likes *itself* in God. It sees *itself* in God, nourishes *itself* with Him, so to speak. Zen Buddhism is free from narcissistic self-reference. There is nothing with which I can melt into one, so to speak, no divine other that reflects my self. No 'God' restores or returns the self. There is no economy of the self to animate the heart that has been emptied. The emptiness of Zen Buddhism negates every form of a narcissistic return to oneself. It *de-reflects* [*ent-spiegelt*] the self. Although Eckhart's soul goes under and sinks *to the ground*, it does not *die to itself* altogether as it does in Zen Buddhism.

Enlightenment (*satori*) does not signify 'rapture' or any unusual 'ecstatic' condition in which one likes one*self*. Rather, it is an *awakening to what is common*. You are awoken not to an extraordinary *There* but to the *age-old Here*, to a deep immanence. The space inhabited by the 'everyday mind' is not Eckhart's divine 'desert'; it is nothing transcendent. Rather, it is a diverse world. Zen Buddhism is inspired by a basic trust in the Here, a basic *trust in the world*. This mental attitude, which knows neither activism nor hedonism, characterizes Far Eastern thought in general. Its trust in the world means that Zen Buddhism is a *world* religion in a very special sense. It knows neither escape from the world nor negation of the world. The Zen saying 'nothing holy' negates any extraordinary, extraterrestrial place. It formulates a *swing back* to the everyday Here.

in the same house
    prostitutes, too, slept:
        bush clover and moon
            – Bashō[81]

The 'emptiness' or the 'nothing' of Zen Buddhism is not a 'desert'. Nor does the path described in *The Ox and His Herdsman* lead into a divine desert landscape. On the ninth picture, we see a tree in bloom. Zen Buddhism lives in the appearing world. Its thinking does not raise itself up to the level of this 'uniform' (*monoeides*), unchanging 'transcendence' but resides in a multiform immanence. The panegyric poem reads: 'Boundlessly flows the river, just as it flows. Red blooms the flower, just as it blooms.'[82] In the final picture of *The Ox and His Herdsman*, on the last stage of the path, a friendly old man comes to the market, that is, to the world of the ordinary. This extraordinary path towards the ordinary can be understood as a walk into immanence.

His face is smeared with earth, his head covered with ashes.
A huge laugh streams over his cheeks.

Without humbling himself to perform miracles or wonders,
he suddenly makes the withered trees bloom.[83]

The 'huge laugh' is a most extreme expression of freedom. It points to a release of the mind: 'It is recounted that Master Yue-shan climbed a mountain one night, looked at the moon and broke into a great laugh that is supposed to have resounded for thirty miles.'[84] Yue-shan laughs *away* every desire, every striving, every attachment, every torpidity and every stiffening; he liberates himself into an unlimited openness without boundaries or obstacles. His laughter *empties* his heart. The mighty laugh flows from the un-bounded, emptied-out and de-internalized mind.

For Nietzsche, too, laughter is an expression of freedom. He *laughs himself free, laughs* any compulsion *to pieces*. Thus, Zarathustra laughs off God: 'You who viewed mankind / As god and sheep –: / *Tearing to pieces* the god in mankind, / Like the sheep in mankind, / And *laughing* while tearing.'[85] Zarathustra tells the 'higher men':[86] 'Lift up your hearts, you good dancers, high! higher! And don't forget good laughter either! / This crown of the laughing one, this rose-wreath crown: to you, my brothers, I throw this crown! I pronounced laughter holy; you higher men, *learn* – to laugh!'[87] A heroism and actionism imbues Nietzsche's laughter with drama. Yue-shan's mighty laugh, by contrast, is neither heroic nor triumphant. Nietzsche's laughter would provoke in Yue-shan another mighty laugh. He would suggest to Zarathustra that he should laugh off his laughter as well; he should *laugh back* into the everyday and the common. He would point out to Zarathustra that, instead of his 'dancers' lifting themselves up to great heights, they should first hop on the ground on which they stand. Nietzsche needs to laugh off not only *theos* but also *anthropos*; the 'overman' needs to laugh himself free, laugh himself off, to become *no one*.

> first snow –
>   just enough to bend
>   narcissus leaves
>   – Bashō[88]

The Chinese Zen master Linji repeatedly calls on his monks to inhabit the Here and Now. His maxim is: 'When you get hungry, eat your rice; when you get sleepy, close your eyes. Fools may laugh at me, but wise men will know what I mean.'[89] The Zen master Enchi Daian is said to have done nothing for thirty years but eat rice.[90] Upon being asked 'What is the most urgent phrase?' Zen Master Yunmen answered: 'Eat!'[91] What word could contain more immanence than 'eat'? The deep sense of 'eat' would be *deep* immanence.

> Looking at bindweed
>   I consume my bowl of rice
>   Such a one I am
>   – Bashō

And the *Shōbōgenzō* likewise says: 'In general, in the house of the Buddhist patriarchs, [drinking] tea and [eating] meals are everyday life itself.'[92] Master Yunmen told the following story:

> A monk said to Master Zhaozhou, 'I have just joined the monastery and am asking for your teaching.' Zhaozhou asked back, 'Have you already eaten your gruel?' The monk replied, 'Yes.' Zhaozhou said: 'Go wash your bowl!'

> Master Yunmen said: 'Well, tell me: was what Zhaozhou said a teaching or not? If you say that it was: what is it that

20

Zhaozhou told the monk? If you say that it wasn't: why did the monk in question attain awakening?'[93]

Case seventy-four of the *Bi-yan-lu* also refers to the spirit of the everyday in Zen Buddhism: 'Every day at mealtime, Jinniu would personally take the rice pail and do a dance in front of the monks' hall; laughing, he would say, "Bodhisattvas, come eat!"'[94]

Eating rice when hungry or sleeping when tired certainly does not mean simply following one's sensual needs or inclinations. The satisfaction of needs requires no mental effort.[95] A long period of exercise, however, is required before it is not one's self but *it* that becomes tired or before one drinks *oneself up*, so to speak, before one ceases to know whether one is the drinker or the tea: 'in complete oblivion of self, self-forlorn: the one who drinks is one with the drink, the drink is one with the one who drinks – an incomparable situation'.[96] When drinking tea, the tea bowl must even be grasped correctly. The goal is a certain mental state in which the hands grasp the bowl as if they were one with it, so that, even when they let go, they retain an imprint of the bowl.[97] And you will have to eat rice until the rice eats you. Or you will have *killed* the rice before you take it in: 'Just as my "I" is empty, all separate entities (*dharmas*) are empty. This applies to all there is, regardless of its kind. . . . what do you call "rice"? Where is there a single grain of rice?!'[98]

> The Master asked a monk, 'Where have you been?'
> The monk replied, 'I've been harvesting tea.'
> The Master asked, 'Do people pick the tea, or does the tea pick people?'
> The monk had no answer.
> In his place, Master Yunmen answered, 'The Master has said it all; there's nothing I can add.'[99]

Dōgen's text *Tenzo Kyokun* (Instructions for the cook), which is dedicated to the daily work of the monastery cook, provides further evidence that the spirit of Zen Buddhism dives into or immerses itself in the everyday. We are faced here with a unique conception of the everyday that lies wholly outside Heidegger's phenomenology of the everyday. The heroism that inspires Heidegger's analysis of Dasein – his ontological term for the human being – sees in the everyday nothing but an 'it's all one and the same', the accustomed, the 'like yesterday, so today and tomorrow':[100]

> 'Everydayness' means the 'how' in accordance with which Dasein 'lives unto the day' [*in den Tag hineinlebt*], whether in all its ways of behaving or only in certain ones which have been prescribed by Being-with-one-another. To this 'how' there belongs further the comfortableness of the accustomed, even if it forces one to do something burdensome and 'repugnant'. That which will come tomorrow (and this is what everyday concern keeps awaiting) is 'eternally yesterday's'.[101]

The everyday is the 'the pallid lack of mood – indifference – which is addicted to nothing and has no urge for anything, and which abandons itself to whatever the day may bring'.[102] Everyday, inauthentic existence is a '[j]ust living along [*Das Dahinleben*] in a way which "lets" everything "be" as it is'.[103] Heidegger calls the Dasein that is fascinated [*benommen*] by everydayness, by the accustomed and ordinary, the 'they' [*das Man*]. The 'they' only exists 'inauthentically'. Its mode of existence is determined by a 'lostness in which it has forgotten itself'.[104] 'Authentic' existence, by contrast, results from a heroic 'resoluteness' to 'choose a kind of Being-one's-Self'.[105] The heroic emphasis on the self liberates Dasein from its 'lostness in which it has forgotten itself', from everydayness, and leads it to authentic existence. Authentic existence differs from the mode of existence of the Zen 'everyday mind', which one might call 'authentic' everydayness or selfless 'authenticity'. This *deep* everydayness is expressed in the Zen saying: 'All is as it was before. "Yesterday, I ate three bowls of rice, this evening five bowls of wheat gruel."'[106] Translated into Heideggerian terminology, the Zen Buddhist formula for enlightenment would be: the 'they' eats. This 'they', however, is the bearer of that 'everyday mind' that is free of any emphasis on the self, on any actionism or heroism.

The everyday time of Zen Buddhism, the time without care [Sorge], does not know that 'moment of vision [*Augenblick*]' that, as the 'extremity' [*Spitze*] of time, as the 'look of resolute disclosedness', breaks through the 'entrancement of time', and does so by emphasizing the self: 'This resolute self-disclosure of Dasein to itself . . . is the moment of vision [*Augenblick*].'[107] The everyday time of Zen Buddhism is a time without 'the moment of vision'. Or: it is a time that consists of moments of everydayness. Without emphatic 'moments', time passes well. It passes well whenever one *happens to dwell* in the gaze of the ordinary.

> Someone asked, 'What is the eye of the genuine [teaching]?'
> Master Yunmen said, 'The steam of rice gruel.'[108]

Enlightenment is an awakening to the everyday. Any searching for an extraordinary *There* leads us astray. What we are after is a leap into the ordinary *Here*: 'Why the search? The ox has never been missing from the beginning.'[109] Instead of moving somewhere else, the gaze should be immersed in immanence. 'We must always look carefully at the spot where our feet are treading, and not lose ourselves gazing into the distance, since wherever we walk or stand the ox always in fact lies under our feet.'[110] The nineteenth koan of the *Mumonkan* says:

23

Joshu asked Nansen, 'What is the Way?' Nansen answered, 'Your ordinary mind, – that is the Way.' Joshu said, 'Does it go in any particular direction?' Nansen replied, 'The more you seek after it, the more it runs away.'[111]

The heart should not strive after anything, not even after 'Buddha'. Striving is exactly what misses the way. The unusual demand of Zen Master Linji, that one should kill Buddha, points to this everyday mind. What is needed is to clear the heart, including of the 'holy'. Unintentional walking is itself the way. With this unintentionality, in such *unique time without concern*, the day passes well.

> One day he said, 'It's eleven days since you entered the summer meditation period. Well, have you gained an entry? What do you say?'
> On behalf of the monks he replied, 'Tomorrow is the twelfth.'[112]

When one has awoken to the everyday mind, '[e]very day is a good day'.[113] The day that passes well is the *deep* everyday that rests in itself. One has to see the unusual in the repetition of the usual, of the age-old. *Satori* leads to a unique repetition. The time of repetition, as a time without concern, promises a 'good time'. The verse of the koan from *Mumonkan* says:

> The spring flowers, the moon in autumn,
> The cool wind of summer, winter's snow, –
> If your mind is not clouded with unnecessary things,
> This is the happy day in human life.[114]

Emptiness

the sea darkening,
a wild duck's call
faintly white
– Bashō[1]

Substance (Latin: *substantia*, Greek: *hypostasis*, *hypokeimenon*, *ousia*) is without a doubt the fundamental concept of occidental thought. According to Aristotle, it denotes what is constant across change. It is constitutive of the unity and self-hood of all beings. The Latin verb *substare* (literally: to stand underneath), from which *substantia* is derived, also means 'to withstand'. *Stare* (to stand) can also mean 'to stand up to, to maintain oneself, to resist'. Thus, the activity of existing and persisting is part of substance. Substance is what remains the same, the identical, that which delimits itself from *the other* by remaining in itself and thus prevailing. *Hypostasis* can mean 'foundation' or 'essence', but it can also mean 'withstanding' and 'steadfastness'. The substance stands firmly by *itself*. The striving towards *itself*, towards self-possession, is inscribed in it. Tellingly, in normal usage *ousia* means 'wealth, possessions, property, estate'. And the Greek word *stasis* not only means 'to stand' but also 'revolt, tumult, quandary, discord, quarrel, enmity' and 'party'. The semantic antecedents of the concept of substance do not at all suggest peacefulness or friendliness, and the concept's meaning is prefigured accordingly. A substance rests on separation and distinction, the delimitation of the one from the other, the holding out of the selfhood of one thing from that of another. 'Substance' is thus conceived with a view not to openness but to closedness.

The central Buddhist concept of *śūnyatā* (emptiness) is in many respects a counter-concept to substance. Substance is *full*, so to speak. It is filled with *itself*, with what is its own. *Śūnyatā*, by contrast, represents a movement of ex-*propriation*. It *empties* out all being that remains within itself, that insists on itself or closes itself up in itself. *Śūnyatā* spills such beings into an openness, into an open, stretched-out distance. Within the field of emptiness, nothing condenses into a massive presence. Nothing rests exclusively on itself. The un-bounding, ex-propriating movement sublates the monadological *for-itself* into a mutual relationship. Emptiness, however, is not a principle of creation; it is not a primary 'cause' from which all beings, all forms, 'emerge'. It has no inherent 'substantial power' that could create an 'effect'. And it is not elevated to a higher order of being by any 'ontological' rupture. It does not mark a 'transcendence' that precedes the forms as they appear. Form and emptiness are situated on the same level of being. There is no gradient of being that separates emptiness from the 'immanence' of the things as they appear. As has often been pointed out, the Far Eastern model of being does not involve 'transcendence' or the 'wholly other'.

Yü-Chien's *Eight Views of the Xiao-Xiang*, inspired by Zen Buddhism, could be interpreted as views of emptiness. They consist of fleeting strokes of the brush that only hint at things, of traces that do not determine anything. The presented forms seem to be cloaked by a peculiar absence. Everything seems inclined to sink back into absence before even truly having appeared. The forms seem to withdraw into the endless expanse of the white background. A certain reserve means that the articulations are kept in a peculiar state of hovering. In their detachment, things float between presence and absence, between being and non-being. They do not express anything final. Nothing imposes itself; nothing delimits itself or closes itself off. Figures blend into each other, follow each other's contours closely, reflect each other, as if emptiness were a *medium of friendliness*. The river sits in its place, and the mountain begins to flow. Earth and sky snuggle up to one another. What is peculiar about this landscape is that the emptiness not only allows the specific shapes of the things to disappear but also allows them to glow in their *graceful* presence. Imposing presences lack grace.

> cuckoo:
> > filtering through the vast bamboo grove
> > the moon's light
>
> > – Bashō[2]

In 'The Sutra of Mountains and Water', Dōgen articulates a particular landscape of emptiness in which 'the Blue Mountains are walking':

> Never insult them by saying that the Blue Mountains cannot walk or that the East Mountain cannot move on water. It is because of the grossness of the viewpoint of the vulgar that they doubt the phrase 'the Blue Mountains are walking'. It is due to the poorness of their scant experience that they are astonished at the words 'flowing mountains'.[3]

The expression 'flowing mountains' is not meant as a 'metaphor'. Dōgen would say that the mountains 'actually' flow. Talk of a 'flowing mountain' would be metaphorical only at the level of 'substance', where the mountain is separate from the water. In the field of emptiness, though, where mountain and water play into each other, that is, at the level of indifference, the mountain 'actually' flows. The mountain does not flow *like* a river; rather the mountain *is* the river. The idea of the difference between mountain and river that we take from the model of substance is sublated here. If we were using metaphor, the river's properties would be merely 'transferred' to the mountains, and the mountains would not 'properly' flow. The mountains would look only *as if* they were moving. Metaphorical speech is thus 'improper'. Dōgen's, by contrast, is neither 'proper' nor 'improper'. It departs from the level of substantial being that makes the separation of 'proper' and 'improper' speech meaningful.

At the level of emptiness, the mountain does not rest in itself like a substance. Rather, it *flows* into the river. A *flowing* landscape unfolds:

> mountains ride the clouds and walk through the sky. The crowns of the waters are mountains, whose walking, upward or downward, is always 'on water'. Because the mountains' toes can walk over all kinds of water, making the waters dance, the walking is free in all directions.[4]

The un-bounded emptiness suspends any rigid opposition: 'Water is neither strong nor weak, neither wet nor dry, neither moving nor still, neither cold nor warm, neither existent nor nonexistent, neither delusion nor realization.'[5] The un-bounding also applies to seeing. The aim is a seeing that takes place prior to the separation of 'subject' and 'object'. The things that are seen do not have a 'subject' imposed upon them. A thing must be seen in the way it sees itself. A certain primacy of the object is meant to protect the object against being appropriated by the 'subject'. Emptiness *empties* the one seeing into what is seen. This is an exercise in a way of seeing that is object-like, a seeing that is becoming object, a seeing that is letting-be, a *friendly* seeing. We need to look at the water the way that water looks at water.[6] Beholding most perfectly would mean the beholder becoming *water-like*. Perfect beholding sees water in its *being-thus*.

Emptiness is a friendly in-difference in which the seer *is* at the same time seen:

> The donkey looks into the well and the well into the donkey. The bird looks at the flower and vice versa. All this is 'concentration in awakening'.
>
> The one nature is present in all beings and they all appear in the one nature.[7]

The bird *is* also the flower; the flower *is* also the bird. Emptiness is the open that allows for mutual permeation. It creates friendliness. One individual being reflects the whole in itself, and the whole dwells in this one being. Nothing withdraws into an isolated *for-itself*.

Everything flows. Things merge into each other and mix together. Water is everywhere:

> To say that there are places not reached by water is the teaching of *śrāvakas* of the Small Vehicle, or the wrong teaching of non-Buddhists. Water reaches into flames, it reaches into the mind and its images, into wit, and into discrimination, and it reaches into realization of the buddha-nature.[8]

The distinction between 'nature' and 'spirit' is suspended. According to Dōgen, water is the body and spirit of the sage.

For the sages who dwell in remote mountains, the mountains are their body and spirit: 'We should remember the fact that mountains are like sages and sages are like mountains.'[9] Zen Buddhist practice lets the monks living in the mountains become mountain-like; they take on the look of the mountain.

The transformation of a mountain into a river would be 'magic'. But magic is the transformation of one substance into another; it does not go beyond the sphere of substance. Dōgen's 'flowing mountains', by contrast, are not the result of a magical transformation of their essence. Rather, they represent an everyday view of an emptiness characterized by the mutual permeation of things:

> There is neither magic, mystery, nor wonder in the real truth. Whoever thinks there is, is on the wrong track. Of course there are all kinds of clever things in Zen, such as making Mount Fuji come out of a kettle, squeezing water out of glowing tongs, putting oneself into a wooden post or changing mountains round. That is nothing magical or wonderful: it is just everyday triviality.[10]

Spring and winter, wind and rain, *dwell* in a plum tree. The tree *is* also the 'heads of patch-robed monks'. But it also withdraws entirely into its fragrance. The field of emptiness is free of any compulsion of identity:

> 'The old plum tree' ... is very unconstrained; it suddenly flowers, and naturally bears fruit. Sometimes it makes the spring, and sometimes it makes the winter. Sometimes it makes a raging wind, and sometimes it makes a hard rain. Sometimes it is heads of patch-robed monks, and sometimes it is eyes of eternal buddhas. Sometimes it has become grass and trees, and sometimes it has become purity and fragrance.[11]

We are not dealing with 'poetic' language here, unless 'poetic' refers to a state of being in which the brace of identity is loosened, that is, to that state of particular in-difference in which speech *flows*. This flowing speech responds to the flowing landscape of emptiness. In the field of emptiness, the things break out of their isolating cells of identity and enter into an all-encompassing unity, the free and unconstrained sphere of mutual permeation. Like the all-pervasive white of snow, the field of emptiness immerses the things in an in-difference. For it is hard to distinguish between the white of blossom and the white of the snow lying on it: 'Snow lies on the panicles of the reeds along the shore; it is difficult to decide where they begin and it ends.'[12] The field of emptiness is in a certain sense un-*limited*. Inside and outside permeate each other: 'In the eyes is snow, in the ears is snow too – just at that moment they are dwelling in uniformity [i.e. in emptiness].'[13]

The 'uniformity' of emptiness *kills* the colours that persist in themselves.[14] But this death at the same time enlivens them. They gain in breadth and depth, or in silence. 'Uniformity' thus has nothing in common with indiscriminate, colourless or monotonous unity. One could say that whiteness, that is, emptiness, is the deep layer or the invisible *breathing space* of colours or forms. Emptiness immerses them in a kind of absence. But this absence also raises them to a special kind of presence. A massive presence that was *only* 'present' would not *breathe*. The mutual permeation of things in the field of emptiness does not bring about a shapeless and formless confusion. It retains the shapes. Emptiness *is* form. 'The Master once said: "True emptiness does not destroy being, and true emptiness does not differ from form."'[15] Emptiness simply prevents what is individual from insisting on itself. It loosens the rigidity of substance. The beings flow into each other without merging into a substance-like 'unity'. In the *Shōbōgenzō* it says:

A person getting realization is like the moon being reflected in water [literally: living or dwelling in water; B-Ch. H.]: the moon does not get wet, and the water is not broken. Though the light [of the moon] is wide and great, it is reflected in a foot or an inch of water. The whole moon and the whole sky are reflected in a dewdrop on a blade of grass and are reflected in a single drop of water. Realization does not break the individual, just as the moon does not pierce the water. The individual does not hinder the state of realization, just as a dewdrop does not hinder the sky and moon.[16]

Emptiness thus does not mean the negation of the individual. Enlightened vision sees every being shining in its uniqueness. And nothing *rules*. The moon is friendly towards the water. The beings dwell in each other without imposing themselves on each other, without hindering each other.

> The bindweed flower
> > Its only calyx breathes
> > > Mountain lake colour . . .
> > > > – Buson

The emptiness or the nothing of Zen Buddhism is therefore not a simple negation of beings, not a formula for nihilism or scepticism. Rather, it represents an utmost affirmation of being. What is negated is only the substance-like delimitation that produces tension. Openness, the friendliness of emptiness, reveals that particular beings are 'in' the world and, further, that the world is in their *foundation*, that in their deep layers they *breathe* the other things and offer them space in which to dwell. In just one thing, then, the whole world dwells.

The fortieth koan of *Mumonkan* runs as follows:

When Isan was with Hyakujo he was the tenzo.[17] Hyakujo wanted to choose a master for Mount Daii, so he called the head monk and the rest of them, and told them that an exceptional person should go there. Then he took a water-bottle, stood it on the floor, and asked a question. 'Don't call this a water-bottle, but tell me what it is.' The head monk said, 'It can't be called a stump.' Hyakujo asked Isan his opinion. Isan pushed the water bottle over with his foot. Hyakujo laughed, and said, 'The head monk has lost.' Isan was ordered to start the temple.[18]

With his answer – that one cannot call a water bottle a 'stump' – the head monk betrayed the fact that he was still attached to thinking in terms of substance: he understood the water bottle in terms of its substance-like identity, which distinguishes it from a stump. The tenzo Isan, by contrast, pushes the water bottle over with his foot, and with this unique gesture, he *empties* out the water bottle; that is, he pushes it into the field of emptiness.

In his famous lecture 'The Thing', Heidegger also approaches a vessel in a very unconventional way:

> How does the jug's void [*Leere*, i.e. emptiness; D. S.] hold? It holds by taking what is poured in. It holds by keeping and retaining what it took in. . . . The twofold holding of the void rests on the outpouring. . . . To pour from the jug is to give. . . . The nature of the holding void is gathered in the giving. . . . We call the gathering of the twofold holding into the outpouring, which, as a being together, first constitutes the full presence of giving: the poured gift. The jug's jug-character consists in the poured gift of the pouring out. Even the empty jug retains its nature by virtue of the poured gift, even though the empty jug does not admit of a giving out. But this nonadmission belongs to the jug and to

33

it alone. A scythe, by contrast, or a hammer is incapable of a nonadmission of this giving.[19]

Thus far, Heidegger has not moved beyond the weak position of the head monk. That monk would also have said: the jug is not a scythe. The 'presence' of the jug, namely the poured gift, is what distinguishes it from scythe and hammer. Heidegger has not yet left behind the model of substance. But he then goes one step further – without, however, pushing over the jug, without pushing it into the field of emptiness:

> The spring stays on in the water of the gift. In the spring the rock dwells, and in the rock dwells the dark slumber of the earth, which receives the rain and dew of the sky. In the water of the spring dwells the marriage of sky and earth. It stays in the wine given by the fruit of the vine, the fruit in which the earth's nourishment and the sky's sun are betrothed to one another. In the gift of water, in the gift of wine, sky and earth dwell. But the gift of the outpouring is what makes the jug a jug. In the jugness of the jug, sky and earth dwell.[20]

The thing is thus not a something with specific *properties*. Rather, the *relations* mediated by 'dwelling' are what makes the jug a jug. Alongside earth and sky, the gods and mortals also dwell in the gift of outpouring:

> The gift of the pouring out is drink for mortals. It quenches their thirst. It refreshes their leisure. It enlivens their conviviality. But the jug's gift is at times also given for consecration. If the pouring is for consecration, then it does not still a thirst. It stills and elevates the celebration of the feast. . . . The outpouring is the libation poured out for the immortal gods. The gift of the outpouring as libation is the authentic

gift. . . . The consecrated libation is what our word for a strong outpouring flow, 'gush', really designates: gift and sacrifice. . . . In the gift of the outpouring that is drink, mortals stay in their own way. In the gift of the outpouring that is a libation, the divinities stay in their own way, they who receive back the gift of giving as the gift of the donation. In the gift of the outpouring, mortals and divinities each dwell in their different ways.[21]

By letting earth and sky, the divinities and the mortals, dwell in itself, that is, by 'gathering' them, the jug *is*. Heidegger calls the 'gathering' of the 'four' the 'world', or the 'fourfold'. The jug *is* the world. The 'essence' of the jug is the relation between earth and sky, between the divinities and the mortals. Although Heidegger thinks the thing from the perspective of these relations between the 'four', he still holds on to the model of 'essence'. The thing is still tied to the figure of substance. In Heidegger's thing there is an inwardness that isolates it, like a monad. On this view, a thing cannot communicate with other things. Each thing, *alone with itself*, gathers earth and sky, divinities and mortals. There is no sense of *neighbourhood*. There is no proximity between things. The things do not dwell or live inside each other. Every thing stands isolated, by itself. Like a monad, Heidegger's thing has no windows. The emptiness of Zen Buddhism, by contrast, creates a neighbourly nearness between things. The things talk to each other, reflect each other. The plum-tree blossom dwells in the pond. The moon and mountain play with each other.

the bell fades away,
the blossoms' fragrance ringing:
early evening

– Bashō[22]

35

Heidegger also tries to think the world in terms of relations. Earth and sky, the divinities and the mortals, are not fixed, substance-like entities. They permeate each other, reflect each other: 'None of the four insists on its own separate particularity. Rather, each is expropriated, within their mutual appropriation, into its own being. This expropriative appropriating is the mirror-play of the fourfold.'[23] Particularly interesting is the expression 'expropriated . . . into its own being' [zu einem Eigenen enteignet]. The expropriation, it follows, does not annul what is proper to a being. It negates only what is beginning to insist on itself, proper-ty [Eigen-tum] that persists in itself. Each of the four finds itself only through the others. It owes what is proper to it to its relations with the others. The relations are older, so to speak, than the 'proper'. The 'appropriation' binds the four into the 'simplicity [Einfalt] of their essential being toward one another'.[24] Internally, however, this simplicity remains a manifold, or rather a fourfold. Each of the four frees itself into its proper own; the simplicity does not involve the properly own being repressed in favour of unity.

The 'world' is not a substance-like something but a relation. In this world relation, the one reflects everything else in itself: 'Each of the four mirrors in its own way the presence of the others. Each therewith reflects itself in its own way into its own, within the simpleness of the four.'[25] The world as 'mirror-play' happens beyond explanatory relations.[26] There are no preceding 'grounds' on which it can be explained. Heidegger therefore draws on a tautological formulation:

The world presences by worlding. That means: the world's worlding cannot be explained by anything else nor can it be fathomed through anything else. This impossibility does not lie in the inability of our human thinking to explain and fathom in this way. Rather, the inexplicable and unfathomable character of the world's worlding lies in this, that causes and grounds remain unsuitable for the world's worlding. . . . The united four are already strangled in their essential nature when we think of them only as separate realities, which are to be grounded in and explained by one another.[27]

None of the four is a separate reality. The world is not a unity that consists of isolated 'substances'. In a certain sense, Heidegger, too, *empties out* the world. The centre of the 'mirror-playing ring' of the 'fourfold' is empty.[28] However, Heidegger does not remain inside this relationality. One could also put it like this: Heidegger does not hold on to relationality, that is, to the absence of substance-like inwardness, until the end. The figure of the 'ring', despite its empty centre, already suggests a certain inwardness. Its closedness, after all, fills the emptiness of the centre with an inwardness. Heidegger's thinking does not remain wholly in relationality or horizontality. This becomes apparent when we look at the figure of God. Beyond the relationality of the world, Heidegger looks *up*. There, in the region of the divinities, is an icon-like window: the divinities are not identical with 'God'; they are arranged around the one 'God', who exceeds the 'relation' of the world. Because of this existence outside of the world, God is able to withdraw into *Himself*, or develop an inwardness. Inwardness, which the 'relation' lacks, is thus reconstituted in the 'He': 'The god, however, is unknown, and he is the measure nonetheless. Not only this, but the god who remains unknown, must by showing *himself* as the one he is, appear as the one who remains unknown.'[29] This inwardness makes it possible to invoke God. As long as it still points to God, the world is not *empty*. The world of Zen Buddhism, which rests on emptiness, is emptied of both *anthropos* and *theos*. This world does not *point* to anything. The impression one gets from Heidegger is that the 'ring' of the world circles around a hidden theological axis. This unique circular movement leads to the emergence of a further inwardness at the 'empty' centre.

Heidegger was probably familiar with the Zen Buddhist figure of emptiness. In his fictional conversation with 'a Japanese', Heidegger has his interlocutor point out that Noh stages are 'empty'.[30] Heidegger then projects his thinking on to this figure of emptiness, ascribing to it an inwardness that is certainly alien to the emptiness of Zen Buddhist teaching. Heidegger uses emptiness to characterize the fundamental figure of his thought, 'being'. 'Being' denotes the 'open' that renders all beings manifest without, however, manifesting itself. Being is not itself one of these beings, but every being owes its meaningful contours to it. Being lets beings be what *each* of them *is*. Being thereby enables every relation to beings. In this context, Heidegger uses the 'jug' as a metaphor for the open of being. According to this metaphor, the 'emptiness', or the 'inner recess',[31] of the jug is more than a result of the shape. For it is not the case that the shape of the jug creates emptiness, a space that is not occupied by anything. Rather, the emptiness is what allows the shape of the jug to emerge in the first place. The emptiness is, so to speak, older than the clay around it. Rather than the emptiness owing its existence to the shaped clay, the shaped clay emerges from the emptiness:

> Yet it must be recognized that the inner recess is not just a haphazard emptiness which arises purely on account of the surrounding walls and which happens not to be full of 'things'. It is just the opposite: the inner recess itself is what determines, shapes, and bears the walling action of the walls and of their surfaces. The walls and surfaces are merely what is radiated out by that original open realm which allows its

openness to come into play by summoning up, round about itself and toward itself, such-and-such walls (the particular form of the vessel). That is how the essential occurrence of the open realm radiates back from and in the embracing walls.[32]

The 'walls' are what is 'radiated out' by emptiness. The open of the 'inner recess' is 'summoning up' the walls 'toward itself'. This 'toward itself' is evidence of the inwardness of this emptiness. Emptiness, the open, is the *soul*, so to speak, of the jug. The shape, or form, would be the radiation emanating from this soul-like inwardness.

For Heidegger, then, emptiness is anything but the absence of something. Rather, it is a dynamic process that, without revealing itself to be 'something', bears, forms, at-*tunes* [be-*stimmt*] and sur-*rounds* every thing, and thereby en-frames all things making them part of a tonal unity. Emptiness manifests as a *ground*-providing mood that at-*tunes* all that is present. The ground-mood binds, gathers, the manifold presences into a comprehensive tonality, into the inwardness of a *voice*. Through this com-prehension, emptiness charts out a place. The place is held and gathered in the gathering and *internalizing* force of emptiness:

> Often enough it appears to be a lack. Emptiness is held then to be a failure to fill up a cavity or gap.
>
> Yet presumably emptiness is closely allied to the special character of place, and therefore not a lacking, but a bringing-forth. Again, language can give us a hint. In the verb 'to empty' [*leeren*] speaks the word 'collecting' [*Lesen*], taken in the original sense of the gathering which rules a place. To empty a glass means: To gather the glass, as that which can contain something, into its having become free. . . .

> Emptiness is not nothing. It is also not a lack. In sculptural embodiment, emptiness plays in the manner of a seeking-projecting instituting of places.[33]

Emptiness empties; that is, it gathers what is presencing into a gathered togetherness of the place. It is what holds together, what 'determines, shapes, and bears', in a way that precedes, however, what it bears and shapes. It is itself invisible, but it shines through all that is visible, allows what is presencing first to shine forth in its meaningfulness. The gathering, at-*tuning* emptiness gives the place an inwardness, a *voice*. It *animates* the place. Heidegger conceives of the place from the perspective of this gathering force:

> Originally the word 'site' [*Ort*] denotes the tip of a spear. Everything comes together in the tip. The site gathers unto itself, to the most supreme and inmost extreme. Its gathering penetrates and pervades everything. The site, the gathering, takes in and preserves all it has taken in, not like an encapsulating shell but rather by penetrating with its light all it has gathered, and only thus releasing it into its own nature.[34]

The 'tip of the spear' that makes everything come together in *itself* illustrates the fundamental movement of inwardness that also determines Heidegger's notion of emptiness. The emptiness of Zen Buddhism, by contrast, does not have a 'tip'. It does not rule in the way of a gathering centre that 'takes in' everything or 'summon[s] up, round about itself and toward itself'. It is emptied of such inwardness and gravity toward-the-self. Precisely the absence of a ruling 'tip' makes it *friendly*. Zen Buddhist teaching is *emptier* than Heidegger's emptiness. One could also say: the emptiness of Zen Buddhism is without *soul* and without *voice*. It is more *scattered* than 'gathered'.

Or: a unique gathering, namely a *gathering without inwardness*, a *mood without voice*, is inherent in it.

> in the plum's fragrance,
> suddenly the sun –
> mountain path
> – Bashō[35]

No one

this road –
with no one on it,
autumn dusk
– Bashō[1]

For Leibniz, the soul is a monad that reflects, or mirrors, the universe in itself. However, this monad does not possess the stillness and selflessness that would make it a friendly echo of the world. Instead, its reflection takes the form of an active *perception*. Inherent in the monad is an 'appetition' (*appetition*, *appetite*, *appetitus*). The Latin verb *appetere* means 'to grasp' for something, 'to seek' something or 'to attack' something. A monad thus perceptually grasps the world. Its perception is a kind of access to the world. A monad has a constant appetite. It strives and desires. *Desire* is the fundamental trait of the *soul*. Its appetite keeps the monad alive, or in existence. The absence of appetite would mean death. *To be* thus means to *have appetite*.

A monad behaves not receptively but expressively. Its world does not actually arise out of passive reflections. Rather, the world is the expression (*expressio*) *of the monad*. By representationally expressing (*exprime*) the world, or the universe, a monad *expresses* itself. In representing the world (*repraesentatio mundi*), a monad represents *itself*. The soul, or monad, *is* what its appetition desires. Desire or the will (*conatus*) constitutes its being.[2] *Appetition* presupposes a kind of *ego*, a kind of *inwardness*, in which 'external things' (*de ce qui est dehors*) are taken up and incorporated like nutrition.[3] The soul, as applied to the human, is only a *someone* as long as it *desires*. A someone *is* what the soul desires and strives for:

> By being representational in this way, a monad presents and represents itself, presents itself and thus represents what it demands in its striving. What it represents in this way, it *is*.
> . . . A man 'represents something' means: he *is* someone.[4]

For Leibniz, the nothing is 'simpler and easier' (*plus simple et plus facile*) than being.[5] In order to be, what is required is a force (*vis*), a will (*conatus*) or an impulse that resists or withstands the nothing. This *capacity to be* consists in a liking-*oneself*, in the 'striving for effecting *oneself*'.[6] Being thus displays the structure of willing to which the self-referentiality of liking-*oneself* is immanent. By contrast, Dōgen's demand that one cast off body and soul refers to that being whose fundamental trait is not willing or desiring. The Zen Buddhist practice makes the heart fast, as it were, until an altogether different being, a being without *appetitus*, becomes accessible to it.

The world of the monad, as an expression of the monad itself, remains locked inside the *interior of the soul*. It lacks an openness. The souls, as windowless individuals, do not look at each other. Every monad stares ahead in self-obsession. Only through 'God's intervention' can they communicate with each other after all.[7] According to Zen Buddhism's conception of the world, by contrast, an un-bounded openness or friendliness is inherent to being, as if it consisted only of windows. Every being reflects all other beings in itself, and those others, in turn, reflect that being: 'One mirror reflects itself in all mirrors, all mirrors reflect each other collectively in one mirror. This reflecting is the reality of the real world.'[8] These reflections take place without desiring, without *appetitus*:

> But what a reflection! And what is it that is reflected in it? There is the earth and the sky; there the mountains rise and waters stream; there the grass becomes green and the trees sprout. And in spring, the flowers bloom in their hundreds. For whom, and why? . . . Is there an intention in all this, a meaning one might find? Is all this not simply there? . . . But only the clear mirror that is *empty in itself*. Only he who has realized the nullity of the world and *of himself* sees the eternal beauty in it.[9]

The mirror in itself is empty. It is fasting; it does not grasp (*appetere*) anything. It reflects without having an inwardness, without desire. If the soul is an organ of desire, then the mirror has no *soul*. It is *no one*, as it were. In its being-no-one, however, it is hospitable towards any being that visits it; the mirror becomes something akin to a guest house. Its emptiness means it is able to host anything: 'We may liken it to a bright mirror which, though it contains no forms, can nevertheless "perceive" all forms. Why? Just because it is free from mental activity.'[10]

> To and fro and to
> The heart, just like a meadow,
> Lets it all happen
>
> – Bashō

Intrinsic to the soul as monad is a perspective from which the world is perceived. The perspectival idea of the world presupposes a point of *striving* from which the world is targeted. Without *appetitus* no perspectival seeing or perspectival grasping of the world is possible. Accordingly, that fasting heart, free of *appetitus*, reflects the world in itself a-perspectivally. It sees the world as it would be seen through itself.

Johann Gottlieb Fichte's treatise *The Vocation of Man* contains an unusual confession of a soul:

> The system of freedom satisfies my heart; the opposite system destroys and annihilates it. To stand, cold and unmoved, amid the current of events, a passive [*träge*] mirror of fugitive and passing phenomena, this existence is insupportable [*unerträglich*] to me; I scorn and detest it. I will love; I will lose myself in sympathy; I will know the joy and the grief of life. I myself am the highest object of this sympathy.[11]

In this passage, the desiring heart is juxtaposed with the 'passive mirror'. The passivity of the mirror is 'unsupportable'; it 'destroys and annihilates' the 'heart'. This obsessional egocentrism represents the fundamental mood of Fichte's soul. The I has a 'drive', a continuing tendency, towards activity, through which it posits itself as an unbounded totality. By contrast, the mirror that is empty in itself is not simply 'passive' or 'ponderous'. Rather, it is *friendly*. Being friendly is neither 'action' nor 'passion'.

> Radiating scent:
> robes, not folded – lying there
> this spring evening
> 　　　　　　　　 – Buson

The constitution of Fichte's soul is monadic. The *appetitus*, the 'striving', is its essential trait. The striving aims to make the world I-like, to make it similar to the I, to determine the Not-I by way of the I. Everything that is not I is merely the material on which the I exercises its force and freedom. The world is meant to become *my* world.

> Going off to sleep
> After the meal – to become
> an ox under plum blossoms
> – Buson

According to Hegel, the soul of an animal possesses more inwardness than that of a flower. Because of its lack of inwardness, he writes, the flower is 'drawn *outward* by the light'. It is not able to persist *in itself*. Its 'self', he adds, 'transitions' 'into light', 'into colourfulness'. Without inner concentration, it shines only *outwardly*. In contrast to flowers, animals, who 'attempt to maintain their selfhood', are characterized by 'duller colours'.[12] Instead, they have their voices, which, as 'real ideality (soul)', represent 'self-movement as a free vibration *within itself*'.[13] This movement is not drawn out of *itself*, not drawn outwards, by the light. It remains within *itself*. Further, Hegel distinguishes between different kinds of bird. The 'birds of the northern lands' lack 'gorgeous colouring' but instead are equipped with more inwardness, a better 'voice'. In the case of 'tropical birds', by contrast, their 'selfhood' is dissolved and drawn out 'into their vegetative covering', their external 'plumage'. They do not sing in a way that audibly expresses inwardness, a deeper soul.[14]

Hegel's notion of spirit, with inwardness being its fundamental trait, is certainly opposed to the Zen Buddhist notion of spirit. Zen Buddhist practice is an attempt at de-*internalizing* spirit without, however, immersing it in, or turning it into, a pure 'outside' and without hollowing it out by reducing it to a 'vegetative covering'. The aim is to empty out the spirit, to make it awake and collected without inwardness. *Satori* may well refer to that state of the spirit in which spirit *flowers*, so to speak, flowers over and away from *itself*, in which it fully turns into light and gorgeous colour. Enlightened spirit *is* the flowering tree. *Satori* is the other of selfhood, the other of inwardness, but it is not an outwardness or alienation. Rather, it involves the overcoming of the distinction between 'inward' and 'outward'. Spirit de-internalizes itself in an in-difference, even in *friendliness*.

> the sun's path –
>   hollyhocks turn with it
>   in summer rains
>   – Bashō[15]

In 'The Japanese Art of Arranged Flowers', the Zen Buddhist philosopher Keiji Nishitani interprets the art of flower arranging from the perspective of the *cutting*. By separating the flower from the root of its *life*, one cuts off its soul. The flower has its instinctual impulse, its *appetitus*, taken away from it. This deals the flower a mortal blow. It makes it *die on its own*. This death, however, differs from withering, which would be a kind of slowly *passing away* [Ab-*leben*], or natural death, for the flower. One hands the flower its death before it has lived its life to the end. In the art of Ikebana, a flower must be removed before it withers, before its natural death, before the living and striving have ceased.

The cut flower, without desire, *lingers there and then*. It fully inhabits the immediate present, without a care for the before or after. All of it becomes time without resisting time. Where it moves along *with* time, is friends with it, time does not pass. Where the striving that finds expression as resistance to time is thrown off, a unique duration emerges *in the midst of* time – a duration without persistence, which does not represent a timeless infinity, or time having been arrested. It is a manifestation of a finitude that rests in itself, bears itself, which does not obliquely look for 'infinity'. Ikebana therefore differs from an art of survival that 'seeks eternity by denying temporality' or by working to remove it.[16] The art of Ikebana is not based on such work of mourning. 'Ikebana' literally means 'making flowers alive'. It is a unique kind of 'making alive'. You make the flower alive, give it a deeper vitality, by handing it its death. Ikebana makes impermanence itself shine, without any semblance of infinity. *Beautiful*, here, is the soothed, calm finitude that rests in itself, a finitude that is illuminated without looking beyond itself. Beautiful is being without *appetitus*.

For Heidegger, the fundamental trait of human Dasein is 'care'. As a 'document' or 'illustration' supporting his thesis, Heidegger quotes an old fable:[17]

Once when 'Care' was crossing a river, she saw some clay; she thoughtfully took up a piece and began to shape it. While she was meditating on what she had made, Jupiter came by. 'Care' asked him to give it spirit, and this he gladly granted. But when she wanted her name to be bestowed upon it, he forbade this, and demanded that it be given his name instead. While 'Care' and Jupiter were disputing, Earth arose and desired that her own name be conferred on the creature, since she had furnished it with part of her body. They asked Saturn to be their arbiter, and he made the following decision, which seemed a just one: 'Since you, Jupiter, have given its spirit, you shall receive that spirit at its death; and since you, Earth, have given its body, you shall receive its body. But since "Care" first shaped this creature, she shall possess it as long as it lives. And because there is

48

now a dispute among you as to its name, let it be called "homo", for it is made out of humus (earth).'[18]

Homo will have to hand *himself* his death in order to become free of care.

On this fable, Heidegger comments as follows:

'Cura prima finxit': in care this entity has the 'source' of its Being. 'Cura teneat, quamdiu vixerit'; the entity is not released from this source but is held fast, dominated by it through and through as long as this entity 'is in the world'. 'Being-in-the-world' has the stamp of 'care' . . . The decision as to wherein the 'primordial' Being of this creature is to be seen, is left to Saturn, 'Time'.[19]

Being is care. In being, I am concerned about *my* being. Care denotes this reference to *oneself*. When I act, I consider the world with regard to *my* possibilities of being. The gaze that looks at the world is not empty. It is occupied by *my* possibilities of being, that is, by the *self*. When I design the interior of a room, for instance, I do so in accordance with one of my possibilities of being. The gaze that looks at the world therefore always has a *direction*. It is steered by my possibilities of being. Only through these possibilities does the world become meaningful for me, or appear in its meaningfulness. Thus, the possibilities of being that I create for my own sake are what articulate the world, give it a meaning, that is, a direction, in the first place. Because I project these possibilities *for my own sake*, the projection [*Entwurf*] of the possibilities of being presupposes a *striving*.[20] Without this original will, the world, for me, *is* not. The *striving*, the *appetitus*, therefore allows the world to *be* for me. Being means striving. Care ultimately means nothing but being striving for something. It is the formula for a human Dasein that exists with an orientation towards *itself*. Heidegger proposes that, 'proximally

49

and for the most part', Dasein is oblivious to this orientation towards itself. That is, it forgets *itself* while living in its thrownness into the world. 'Proximally and for the most part', Dasein's existence is 'inauthentic'.[21] The authenticity of existence comes about when Dasein, against the everyday loss of self, takes hold *of itself* in ownmost fashion [*eigens*]. Authentic existence requires a 'resoluteness' in choosing a 'kind of "Being-one's-Self"'.[22] An *I-am* must be able to accompany all my possibilities of being. This pronounced relation to self is not, however, an egotistic self-centredness, because it is also possible to take up or choose altruistic actions as one's possibility of being. In this case, too, one chooses, *in ownmost fashion, oneself.* Thus, the emphasis on the self can also be the accompaniment of *heroic* love.

The projection of Dasein is a matter of 'one's own factual freedom' or of 'the way in which I exist freely'.[23] A projection, as freedom, remains tied to the striving of a self. Dasein projects *itself* towards a possibility of being. The projection of the *possibilities* of being discloses the future. Dasein exists in a future tense, as it exists by projecting possibilities of *itself*. The future, which is *my* projection, reflects my own self back to me. It is my representation. The future is the 'the coming in which Dasein, in its ownmost potentiality-for-Being, comes towards itself'.[24] The '"towards-oneself" (to oneself!)' is the fundamental trait of the future.[25] The future arises out of willing-oneself and projecting-oneself. The priority of the future points towards the priority of the self. Care, as care about oneself, articulates time as a *time of the self.* Care is mainly concerned about the future. The future is the *head of time*, so to speak. Time without care, by contrast, would be a whiling in each present.

Come, let's go to bed!
   The new year is a matter
   Of another day
            – Buson

Care is the centre of gravity of Heidegger's Dasein. Care is what makes Dasein perpetually circle around *itself*. The Zen Buddhist practice is instead to cast off this heaviness of the *self*, that is, to be *without care*, to perceive the world in its being-thus without care of *self*. In the *Shōbōgenzō* it says: 'To practice and confirm all things by conveying one's self to them, is illusion; for all things to advance forward and practice and confirm the self, is enlightenment.'[26]

> Not yet become a Buddha,
>   this ancient pine tree,
>   dreaming.
>
> – Issa[27]

The human being without care does not guard an *I-am*. Instead of seeking to remain identical to itself, it transforms itself in accordance with the course of things. It is as it were like a no one, a selfless self that simply reflects things. It is a human being that shines in the light of things. To Faust's complaint that he houses two souls in himself,[28] Bashō might have said: cut out your souls and let a plum tree flower in their place.

Art inspired by Zen Buddhism is always based on a unique experience of transformation. One Zen saying goes: 'Having exhaustively considered the landscape Xiao-Xiang, I enter the painted picture with a boat.'[29] To consider a landscape exhaustively does not mean to comprehend it in its entirety. Comprehending an object in its entirety would mean fully taking possession of it. Considering a landscape exhaustively, however, would mean looking away from *oneself* and becoming immersed in the landscape. The beholder then does not have the landscape in front of *himself* as an ob-ject. Rather, the beholder fuses with the landscape. About the painting *Evening snow in the countryside, where river and sky*

51

blend into each other, Yü-Chien says: 'The endless expanse of river and sky is the endless expanse of the heart.'[30] The heart here is not an organ of inwardness. It beats in the *outward world*. Its expanse is coextensive with the expanse of the landscape. River and sky blend into each other and flow into the de-internalized, emptied-out heart of the *no one*.

Yü-Chien frames his painting *Sailing boats return to the distant bay* with the following words:

> Unbounded land enters the tip of the brush. Sails have fallen into the autumnal river and are hidden in the evening haze. The last glow of dusk has not yet disappeared, but the lamps of the fishermen already begin to shimmer. Two old men in a boat talk placidly about the land of Jiangnan.[31]

This landscape is un-*bounded* because it *flows*. The evening haze conceals the sails. The boat can hardly be distinguished from the autumnal river. Light and dark mingle. And where the unbounded land enters the tip of the brush, the painter *is* the landscape. He paints *himself away* into the landscape. The painter reflects the landscape in himself, as if he were no one. The landscape paints the landscape, leading the brush. The landscape is seen as it sees itself, without a perspective introduced by the observing painter. The brush that becomes one with the landscape does not allow for the kind of distance that a perspectival, reifying seeing requires. And where unbounded land fuses with the tip of the brush, every brushstroke *is* the whole landscape. Every brushstroke breathes the whole – the whole landscape of Xiao-Xiang. In Zen Buddhist landscape painting, nothing is actually painted, or executed, as such. There is no discursive amassing or collecting of parts into a whole.

Transformation is also an important element in the Japanese Noh theatre, a deeply religious form of dramatic art made up of music and dance, narration and singing, silk robes and wooden masks. The stage looks like a small temple without front or side walls. The backdrop is the mirror wall, a back wall with a painting of an old pine tree, which looks like a silent reflection of the world. At the rear on the left-hand side, the stage opens onto a bridge lined with pine trees, across which the Noh players enter the stage. The bridge connects the stage to a room called the 'mirror room', which has a large mirror on the wall. The mirror room could be described as a holy space of transformation. Here, the main character of a Noh play, the *shite*, collects himself before the performance.[32] In front of the mirror, he puts on the Noh mask, the *omoto*, and undergoes the transformation. He transforms himself into the face of the mask that he sees in the mirror. In front of the mirror, the actor empties himself out of himself, passing over into the *other*. He gathers himself into the other. The mirror is not a narcissistic space but a space of transformation.

The Noh mask itself has something indeterminate about it. Its expression is multi-layered and complex. Because of this inscrutable, indeterminate expression, the mask's expression is not fixed. Its beauty, or grace, lies precisely in the peculiar way in which it *hovers* between expressions. Through imperceptible movements of the head, through the play of light and shadow, an actor produces now this expression, now that. Apart from some of the demon masks, the Noh masks appear *dull*, devoid of expression, but just because of this emptiness they are capable of taking on many expressions. The Noh mask also appears to hover because it seems to be situated in a space between dream and reality.

Once Zhuang Zhou dreamed he was a butterfly, a butterfly flitting and fluttering around, happy with himself and doing as he pleased. He didn't know he was Zhuang Zhou. Suddenly he woke up, and there he was, solid and unmistakable Zhuang Zhou. But he didn't know if he were Zhuang Zhou who had dreamed he was a butterfly or a butterfly dreaming he was Zhuang Zhou.[33]

Even in Noh plays performed without masks, the faces of the actors remain, in a peculiar way, as empty as the masks. Even their expressions of emotion are not expressive. The Noh dancing, too, at first appears expressionless. It mainly consists of dragging and sliding movements (*mau*) on the stage floor, in which the soles of the feet hardly leave the ground. After a slight lifting of the toes, the feet gently and silently touch and follow the floor again. The dancer's body stays mostly in touch with the ground. There are no leaps or heroic displays that disrupt the contact between the floor and the feet of the dancer.[34]

In the same way, haikus and Zen poems are not *expressions* of the *soul*. They can rather be interpreted as *views of the no one*. It is not possible to detect any inwardness in them. They do not express a 'lyrical I'. In a haiku, the things are *pushed towards nothing*. The things are not flooded by a 'lyrical I' that seeks to turn them into metaphors or symbols. Rather, a haiku lets the things shine in their being-thus. Being-pushed-towards-nothing, as the fundamental mood of the haiku, points to the fasting heart of the poet, reflecting the world as a *no one*.

Onto the duck's wings
   The soft snow falls and piles up
     Oh, this great stillness
          – Shiki

Although haikus do not involve a human individual, an 'I', who takes up the word, they nevertheless do not belong in the neighbourhood of the impersonal 'it poem' that Heidegger tries to interpret from the perspective of the 'event'. In *On Time and Being*, Heidegger quotes from Georg Trakl:

> It is a light which the wind has extinguished.
> It is a jug which a drunkard leaves in the afternoon.
> It is a vineyard, burned and black with holes full of spiders.
> It is a room which they have whitewashed with milk.
> . . .
> It is a stubble field on which a black rain falls.
> It is a brown tree which stands alone.
> It is a hissing wind which circles around empty huts.
> How sad this evening.[35]

Heidegger stresses the closeness of the 'it is' to the 'there is' (*il y a*) in a poem by Rimbaud:

> Au bois il y a un oiseau, son chant vous arrête et vous fait rougir.
> Il y a une horloge qui ne sonne pas.
> Il y a une fondrière avec un nid de bêtes blanches.
> Il y a une cathédrale que descend et un lac qui monte.
> [In the woods there's a bird whose singing stops you and makes you blush.
> There's a clock which doesn't strike.
> There's a clay-pit with a nest of white animals.
> There's a cathedral coming down and a lake going up.][36]

The ordinary 'there is' [*Es gibt*], Heidegger says, always expresses a relation to a being, a relation that points towards the being's appropriation by man:

If we say, for example, there are trouts in the brook, the mere 'Being' of trouts is not being confirmed. Before that, and at the same time, a distinction of the brook is expressed in this sentence. The brook is characterized as a trout brook, thus as a special brook, one in which we can go fishing. In the simple use of 'It gives', 'there is', there already lies the relation to man.

This relation is usually that of being available, the relation to a possible appropriation by man.[37]

Oh, what a coolness:
  Evening, the tide swells up
  And fish are jumping
            – Shiki

By contrast, Heidegger continues, Trakl's 'it is' (*'Es ist'*) and Rimbaud's 'there is' (*'Il y a'*) do not 'name the availability of something which is, but rather something unavailable, something that concerns us as uncanny, the demonic', which is inaccessible to humans.

Haikus give voice to the world, to things in their being-thus, which shines beyond human access. But this being-thus does not manifest itself as a demonic, impersonal 'it'. It is *friendly* rather than demonic or uncanny. In contrast to 'it poems', haikus do not really *refer* to anything, do not refer to an unavailable *noun*. The I and the world are not flooded by a demonic 'it'. If we consider them more closely, it becomes clear that 'it poems' still harbour an I that, left without any meaningful relation to the world, is exposed to the world as an impersonal, anonymous entity. In the things named by the 'it poem', we can hear the voice of an alienated and hollow I, wandering around worldless, seeking and calling. The things in these poems do not communicate with one another. Each thing becomes an empty, anonymous echo of the 'it'. The 'it

56

poems' are marked by a complete lack of relation, whereas haikus articulate relationality, a friendly being-in-relation.

Emptiness, the site of the haiku, empties out the I as well as the 'it'. Haikus are thus neither 'personal' nor 'impersonal'.

> the stench of the stone –
> > the summer grass red,
> > > the scorching dew
> > > > – Bashō[38]

Haikus do not have hidden meanings that must be uncovered. There are no metaphors that need to be interpreted. In a haiku, everything is *fully revealed*. It is as such *bright*. It does not first need to be 'illuminated'.

> A gust of wind
> whitens
> > the water birds.
> > > – Buson[39]

Haikus completely reveal their 'meaning'. They have nothing to hide. They are not turned inward. There is no 'deep meaning' inherent in them. This absence of 'deep meaning' is precisely what makes for the *profundity* of haikus, a profundity that corresponds to the absence of soul-like inwardness. The haiku's bright openness, its unobstructed expanse, originates in the de-internalized, emptied-out heart, the inwardness-free concentration of the no one.

Dwelling nowhere

Sick on a journey,
my dreams wander
the withered fields.
– Bashō[1]

Bashō's travel diary *The Narrow Road to the Deep North* (*Oku no Hosomichi*) begins with the following words:

'The days and months are travellers of eternity, just like the years that come and go.' For those who pass their lives afloat on boats, or face old age leading horses tight by the bridle, their journeying is life, their journeying is home. And many are the men of old who met their end upon the road.

How long ago, I wonder, did I see a drift of cloud borne away upon the wind, and ceaseless dreams of wandering become aroused?[2]

The quotation opening his diary is taken from the prelude to a poem by the Chinese poet Li Po, *The Spring Evening Banquet in the Peach and Pear Blossom Garden*:

> Heaven and earth – the whole cosmos – is just a guest-house;
>   it hosts all beings together.
> Sun and moon are also just guests in it, passing guests in
>   eternal times.
> Life in this fleeting world is like a dream.
> Who knows how many more times we are going to laugh?
> Our ancestors therefore lit candles in praise of the night.[3]

For Bashō, 'wind' is a synonym for wandering and for the fleetingness of things. He understands himself as an 'itinerant monk whose robes flutter in the wind'. The literal meaning of the term 'fūryū', used by Bashō to describe his poetry, is 'wind-flow'.[4] Bashō might also have said 'poetically man dwells'. For him, dwelling poetically would mean dwelling nowhere, like drifting clouds, *in every place sojourning* as a guest of the world, which is a guest house. Hiking along with the wind would be a unique form of dwelling, one that is on friendly terms with finitude. You dwell in, walk through, finitude.

> We returned to the shore and found lodgings, a second-storey room with open windows that looked out over the bay. As we lay there in the midst of breeze and cloud, I felt a marvellous exhilaration. Sora wrote:

> Matsushima, oh . . .
>   you will need cranes' wings to fly
>   little cuckoo bird.[5]

Bashō's constant wanderings are an expression of his fasting heart, which does not cling on to anything, does not sink its teeth into anything. In a letter, Bashō gives voice to his heart's desire:

> As I very much wish to live like the drifting clouds with a heart that dwells nowhere, I beg you to accommodate my wish while I am wandering around. Please, do only procure for me those things to which I do not need to become attached, and to which my heart will not be committed too much. As I think of my provisional sojourn as being like a spider's web that is exposed to the way the wind blows, the place may be an (unassuming) small house, but at the same time for me it isn't only that.[6]

> say something
>   and the lips go cold:
>   autumn wind
>   – Bashō[7]

Bashō's hiking is not a relaxed, leisurely walking. Rather, it is a wandering without *slowness* [*Gemach*],[8] a constant, painful leave-taking.

> departing spring –
>   birds cry, in the fishes'
>   eyes are tears . . .
>   – Bashō[9]

> The blossoms I mourn
>   the fleeting world – before me
>   just dull wine, black rice . . .
>   – Bashō

Bashō's mourning, however, does not have the oppressive heaviness of melancholy. Rather, it brightens up and turns into serenity. This bright, serene mourning is the fundamental mood of his heart, which, bidding its farewells, dwells nowhere. It is a mood that differs fundamentally from a mourning that is closed up in itself and that labours hard to get over the farewells and over impermanence, to expel time.

> a sick goose
>> falling in the night's cold:
>>> sleep on a journey . . .
>>>> – Bashō[10]

It is likely that Bashō was familiar with the *Diamond Sutra*, which talks about the heart that is the result of dwelling nowhere, of being based nowhere:[11] 'A Zen monk should be like a cloud with no fixed abode, like flowing water with nothing to rely on.'[12] Hiking, as a form of dwelling nowhere, does not hold on to anything. It concerns not only the relation to the world but also the relation to oneself. Dwelling nowhere means not holding on to oneself, not remaining within oneself, that is, letting oneself go, turning away from oneself – and, in the midst of transience, letting *oneself* pass too. Such equanimity [*Gelassenheit*] is the constitution of the heart that dwells nowhere.[13] Hiking also means hiking *oneself away*. The one who dwells nowhere is not at home in his *self*. Rather, he is a guest there. All forms of possession and self-possession are renounced. Neither body nor mind is *mine*.[14]

The house that one must leave in order to dwell nowhere is not a simple shelter. It is the place of the soul and of inwardness, where I enjoy myself and in which I wrap myself up, a space of my *being-able-to* and my *potential* in which I possess *myself* and *my* world. The I depends on the possibility of possession and collecting. The *oikos* (the house) is the place of this economic existence. Dwelling nowhere is therefore opposed to the economic world, to the household.

Heidegger's analysis of Dasein also identifies an essentially economic form of existence. The 'existence' of Dasein is tied to the *oikos*; it is economic 'existence'. Heidegger could have introduced the house as a mode of being for Dasein, that is, as an 'existential'. Dasein perceives the world only with regard to *itself*, to its own possibilities of being. 'Being-in-the-world' ultimately means being-at-home-with-oneself. 'Care', as care for *oneself*, would be the constitutive state of the house understood as an 'existential'. Dasein is incapable of wandering.

The heart that dwells nowhere is opposed to the kind of subject whose fundamental trait is the continual return to itself, the subject that is always at home with *itself*. For this subject, every turn towards the world is a return to itself. When it steps towards the world, it does not gain any distance from itself. In everything it knows, it is aware of itself. An I-am accompanies all of its ideas. The certainty of being depends on the certainty of self. Levinas compares this subject to Ulysses. It possesses an 'autonomy of consciousness, which finds itself again in all its adventures, returning home to itself like Ulysses, who through all his peregrinations is only on the way to his native island'.[15] Levinas juxtaposes the economic existence of Ulysses with 'the story of Abraham who leaves his fatherland forever for a yet unknown land'.[16]

Is Abraham really free of economic existence? Genesis recounts that he leaves the house of his father but still holds on to his possessions and his family. Abraham sets off into an unknown elsewhere, but his departure does not mark an interruption of his economic existence:

> So Abram departed, as the LORD had spoken unto him; and Lot went with him: and Abram *was* seventy and five years old when he departed out of Haran. And Abram took Sarai his wife, and Lot his brother's son, and all their substance

that they had gathered, and the souls that they had gotten in Haran; and they went forth to go into the land of Canaan; and into the land of Canaan they came.[17]

The departure or exodus is ultimately a removal, a change of house in which Abraham takes his possessions and souls with him. He is, of course, not going to be led astray by God. His separation from the house of his father is bound up with the promise of a new, richly appointed house:

> Now the LORD had said unto Abram, Get thee out of thy country, and from thy kindred, and from thy father's house, unto a land that I will shew thee: And I will make of thee a great nation, and I will bless thee, and make thy name great; and thou shalt be a blessing: And I will bless them that bless thee, and curse him that curseth thee: and in thee shall all families of the earth be blessed.[18]

And God repeats his promise. The world Abraham sees all around him is destined to become *his* world:

> Lift up now thine eyes, and look from the place where thou art northward, and southward, and eastward, and westward: For all the land which thou seest, to thee will I give it, and to thy seed for ever. And I will make thy seed as the dust of the earth: so that if a man can number the dust of the earth, *then* shall thy seed also be numbered. Arise, walk through the land in the length of it and in the breadth of it; for I will give it unto thee. Then Abram removed *his* tent, and came and dwelt in the plain of Mamre, which *is* in Hebron, and built there an altar unto the LORD.[19]

Abraham is certainly *interested* in the possessions he is promised, so he asks God for certainty, for a visible sign:

And he said unto him, I *am* the LORD that brought thee out of Ur of the Chaldees, to give thee this land to inherit it. And he said, Lord GOD, whereby shall I know that I shall inherit it?[20]

Abraham's faith does not mark an interruption of economic existence. Even the sacrifice of Isaac is not entirely free from calculation. Abraham will have thought: 'But it will not happen, or if it does, the Lord will give me a new Isaac.'[21]

Dwelling nowhere, wandering, presupposes a radical renunciation of possession, of what is *mine*. Bashō walks *himself* and his possessions away. He cancels his economic existence altogether. His wandering does not aim at a promised future. The temporality of his hiking is without future. Bashō's wandering is *in the moment*; it rests in the presence of each moment. His wandering is free of any teleological or theological meaning. Bashō has *always already arrived*. We might see this itinerant monk, his robes fluttering in the wind, as a figure that is opposed to Ulysses and Abraham. Bashō is hiking because he *strives* to be nowhere. Ulysses' odyssey, by contrast, presupposes his return. It has a direction. Abraham, like Ulysses, is not a wanderer because, like Moses, he is on his way to his promised home.

> travel weary,
>> just as I finally find lodging –
>> wisteria blossoms
>>> – Bashō[22]

Dwelling nowhere radically questions the paradigm of identity. The heart is not filled with a striving for the immutable:

> The mind changes, following along with ten thousand
> environments;

the way it changes is truly most mysterious.
If you follow its flow and can perceive its nature,
you will have neither joy nor sorrow.[23]

The heart that dwells nowhere, that does not cling on to any-thing, follows the changing circumstances. It does not remain identical with itself. Dwelling nowhere is a *mortal* form of *dwelling*. In its detachment, the heart is not tied to anything, and it knows neither joy nor sorrow, neither love nor hate. The heart that dwells nowhere is too *empty*, so to speak, to be capable of love or hate, joy or sorrow. The freedom of detachment represents a unique in-difference [*In-Differenz*]. In this in-*difference* [Gleich-*Gültigkeit*], the heart is friendly to all that comes and goes.[24]

Hiking, or dwelling nowhere, was certainly alien to Plato, for whom one does not leave the house even after death. In the *Apology*, Socrates speaks of death as a 'relocating for the soul' (*metoikesis*); death is 'a change [*metabole*] and a relocating for the soul from here to another place'.[25] The 'transforma-tion' (*metabole*) the soul undergoes in death does not render it *homeless*. This relocation or removal is not a wandering. The soul leaves one house (*oikos*) in order to arrive at another. Death is a relocation from one house to another. For Bashō, by contrast, to die is to wander.

For Plato, death is an undertaking of the 'soul', which departs from the finite house of the body to a heavenly abode. If the soul 'leaves the body' after having '*gathered itself together by itself*' in life,[26] it need not fear 'that, on parting from the body, the soul would be scattered and dissipated by the winds and no longer be anything anywhere [*oudamou*]'.[27] The gath-ering or inwardness of the soul facilitates its relocation to its new heavenly home. The house to which this gathered soul is on its way is better than the house it has left behind. It is the place of the 'pure and uniform [*monoeides*]', where no transformation, no change, no metamorphosis takes place, where everything remains identical with itself.[28] The heavenly house guards identity. What cannot be called *homely* is the mind that 'changes, following along with ten thousand environments', constantly shifting like water.

> In wandering clothes
>> A crane flies in winter rain
>>> The master Bashō
>>>> – Chora

The inwardness of the hearth is not alien to the gods. For the house of the gods is guarded by Hestia, the goddess of the hearth, while other gods 'patrol all of heaven'.[29] Hestia *stays at home*. The patrolling of the gods is not a wandering. The Platonic gods do not wander. They always return 'home' (*oikade*); they 'sink back inside [*to eiso*] heaven and go home'.[30]

Plato's *Republic* could also be read as a book for householders, as a book on housekeeping. The dialogue describes an economic form of existence. Plato's criticism of poetry is at the same time a criticism of wandering and metamorphosis. Plato denies entry to his polis to the 'holy, wonderful, and pleasing [*hedys*]'[31] poet, 'who through clever training [*hypo sophias*] can become anything [*pantodapon*] and imitate anything'.[32] He has the poet wander outside the polis. Plato would probably have been very irritated by the loud laughter of the Zen masters: he prohibits the poetic representation of laughter. Laughter, he thinks, causes 'a violent change of mood' which places us *outside of ourselves*.[33]

The fasting heart, dwelling nowhere, certainly does not cling to the body. Indeed, it is liberated not only from bodily desire but from desire as such. Not just the body but the soul too is emptied out. The Platonic soul, by contrast, is characterized fundamentally by desire. The metaphor of the 'wings' that lift the soul to heaven is an illustration of the soul's inner constitution.[34] This metaphor is dominated by an opposition between *below* and *above*. The soul desires the 'divine' (*theion*), the 'immortal' (*athanaton*).[35] Emptiness, however, cannot be an object of desire, for it is a *nothing*. It empties out all desire. Further, it belongs to the everyday rather than to the 'divine'. Nor can it be called 'uniform' (*monoeides*), because it is emptied of all form (*eidos*). There is no form to impede the freedom from all attachment. Emptiness, however, is not the wholly other of the multiform, manifold world. It *is* the world. It is not as if there were a ladder of being between emptiness and the multiform world. One does not hike out into a transcendence; one wanders within everyday immanence.

To dwell nowhere is not to flee from the world. It is not the negation of dwelling in *this* world. The awakened one does not prowl a desert of nothingness. Rather, 'he stands in the midst of the throng on the busy road and in spite of it never turns away from his original self'.[36] Dwelling nowhere is still dwelling, but it is one that is without desire, without a firmly closed-up self. It is a dwelling that does not turn its back on the world. The emptiness is an articulation of a specific 'no', but the Zen Buddhist path does not end with this 'no'. It leads back to a yes, namely the inhabited, multiform world. That 'yes' is the deep meaning of the Zen saying quoted, in part, above: 'All is as it was before. "Yesterday, I ate three bowls of rice, this evening five bowls of wheat gruel." Each being, as it is, is affirmed with a great "yes".'[37] This double movement of 'no' and 'yes' is also expressed in the following passage:

Before we were awakened the mountain was just a mountain and the river just a river. When we were once suddenly awakened, by training with a master who had insight, the mountain was not the mountain and the river was not the river; the willow was not green and the flower was not red.

If we go further along the way of ascending and succeed in reaching the 'ground and origin' then the mountain is the mountain, the river is the river, the willow is green and the flower is red, through and through. 'Complete awakening is like not-yet-awakening', in spite of the great fundamental difference.[38]

Dwelling nowhere implies a 'yes' to dwelling. But this dwelling has gone through the 'no' of nowhere, or emptiness – through death. The world is 'substantially' the same, but it has become *lighter* by as much as the weight of emptiness, as it were. That emptiness turns dwelling into wandering. Thus, dwelling nowhere does not simply negate the house and dwelling. Rather, it opens up a primordial dimension of dwelling. It lets you dwell without being at home with *yourself*, without you enclosing yourself in your home, without clinging on to yourself or your possessions. It opens the house, gives it a friendly atmosphere. The house thereby loses the aspect of housekeeping, the narrowness of the interior and of inwardness. *It de-internalizes itself into a guest house.*

Death

The petals flutter
down. With each the branch of the
plum tree grows older
                              – Buson

In his lectures on Hegel, Heidegger remarks that Hegel does not know death, that death for him 'can never become a serious threat; no καταστροφή is possible, nor is any downfall and subversion [*Sturz und Umsturz*] . . . Everything is *already unconditionally* secured and accommodated.'[1] But has there ever been a philosophy that has viewed death as the 'catastrophe' par excellence? Could it ever be possible simply to observe decline and decay? To refrain from turning the infinite muteness, the mute nothing, into an eloquent being, to avert the catastrophe (Greek: overturning, reversal), this misery?

His sleeping form –
I shoo away the flies today.
There's nothing more to do.

As the day drew to a close, I vainly tried to wet his lips with water from a vessel at his bedside. The twentieth-night moon shone in through the window, and all the neighborhood was sleeping quietly. As a cock's crow could be heard in the distance announcing the dawn, Father's breathing became increasingly shallow, so shallow that it could hardly be heard.[2]

For Plato, death was not a catastrophic final moment but a significant turning point towards a higher form of being. Death brings the soul closer to the 'invisible', the 'divine', the 'intelligible', the 'uniform', which, being 'indissoluble', is 'always the same as itself'.[3] In Plato, philosophy stands in a unique relation to death, because death is not just one of philosophy's objects. Philosophy means dying. On this uniquely intimate relationship between death and philosophy, Plato remarks: 'I am afraid that other people do not realize that the one aim of those who practice philosophy in the proper manner is to practice for dying and death.'[4] Death, however, is not not-being. Rather, death elevates, intensifies, transfigures being. For the soul that in life had 'gathered itself together by itself' – undistracted and not confused by the body, which blurs the truth – to be dead means to be awake.[5] Death intensifies the gathering and inwardness of the soul. Philosophizing as dying means killing off the bodily or sensual in favour of the invisible and intelligible:

for if it is impossible to attain any pure knowledge with the body, then one of two things is true: either we can never attain knowledge or we can do so after death. Then and not

70

before, the soul is by itself apart from the body. While we live, we shall be closest to knowledge if we refrain as much as possible from association with the body and do not join with it more than we must, if we are not infected with its nature but purify ourselves from it until the god himself frees us. In this way we shall escape the contamination of the body's folly; we shall be likely to be in the company of people of the same kind, and by our own efforts we shall know all that is pure, which is presumably the truth.[6]

A philosopher must bear death in mind. Caring about philosophy means caring about death. The philosopher must die within life, must, while living, anticipate death by fleeing and despising the body as the place of evil and finitude. Death is thus not an end point, not a downfall or subversion, but a particular kind of beginning, a point of departure from which the soul, liberated from the burden of the body, rises with ease like a butterfly to a 'noble and pure and invisible' place.[7]

> should I take it in my hand
> > it would melt in these hot tears:
> > > autumn frost
> > > > – Bashō[8]

According to Hegel, all that is particular or finite must perish because it is not the general or infinite. The 'disparity between its finitude and universality' is 'the inborn germ of death'.[9] But death does not cast the particular into nothingness. Rather, the particular is sublated into the general; it is elevated and transfigured. Death is a 'conversion of bodily and spiritual individuality into its essence and universality'. It is not an endpoint but a 'point of transition'.[10] The particular does not *vanish*; it *goes down* [geht *zu Grunde*]. Death is therefore not a catastrophe. It is a turn and reversal to a higher form of being, a 'return' of the negative to the positive. Death *brings* the finite to the *ground*.[11] In death, the particular casts off its finitude and approaches its infinite ground. Hegel's understanding of death is influenced by the Platonic model. Death promises infinity: 'The finite is determined as the negative, it must free itself from itself. This first natural, simple self-emancipation of the finite from its finiteness is death.'[12]

Hegel's understanding of death is inspired by heroism. 'However, the life of spirit is not a life that is fearing death and austerely saving itself from ruin; rather, it bears death calmly, and in death, it sustains itself', Hegel says. The power of spirit does not consist of the purely positive but in the fact that it is 'looking the negative in the face and lingering with it'. From this heroic being unto death, he continues, emanates the 'magical power that *converts it* [i.e. the negative] *into being*'.[13] Spirit is not shaken by death. Spirit's heroism rather consists in practising its force on death, on the negative.

For Fichte, too, death is not an endpoint but a beginning and birth:

All Death in Nature is Birth, and in Death itself appears visibly the exaltation of Life. There is no destructive principle in Nature, for Nature throughout is pure, unclouded Life; it is not Death which kills, but the more living Life, which, concealed behind the former, bursts forth into new development.[14]

Nature is incapable of killing the I because it 'only exists for me, and for the sake of me', and it 'exists not if I am not'. 'Exactly because she destroys me', Fichte goes on, 'must she animate me anew; it can only be my Higher Life, unfolding itself in her, before which my present life disappears; and what mortals call Death is the visible appearance of a second animation.'[15] Death is no more than 'the ladder by which my spiritual vision rises to a new Life and a new Nature'.[16] Thus '*my* death' is ultimately not possible.[17] Nor can 'my spirit ... regard [the other] as annihilated'; 'he is still, and to him belongs a place' because he is 'my brother'. We 'mourn for him' only 'here below' – 'above there is rejoicing' because 'sorrow shall remain behind in the sphere I shall have left'. Fichte's labour of mourning, as a labour against the finite, kills my *own* death as well as the death of the other. It turns death back into life, reverses the catastrophe. Fichte's mourning is compulsive; it does not liberate itself to become a serene letting go [*gelassene Heiterkeit*]. His 'rejoicing' appears equally compulsive, and strangely rigid; his peroration runs: 'Thus do I live, thus am I, and thus am I unchangeable, firm, and completed for all Eternity.'[18]

> Old lazy-bones –
> slowly roused from a nap by
> falling spring rain
> — Bashō[19]

Heidegger's remark that Hegel does not view death as a 'catastrophe' prompts the question of how far Heidegger understood death as a 'catastrophe'. What kind of 'downfall' or 'subversion' does death bring with it for Heidegger? The word 'catastrophe' does not occur in the analysis of death in *Being and Time*. Death, however, is said to represent a 'measureless impossibility of existence'.[20] What does 'measureless' mean here? Does the term refer to the catastrophic character of death, to the fact that it casts being into its absolute opposite, namely nothingness?

In another passage, Heidegger calls death an 'uttermost possibility' of Dasein, namely the possibility of Dasein 'giving itself up'.[21] What is striking here is that he understands death as an activity. Dasein gives itself up. Death is therefore not something that 'Dasein' is forced, at some point, to suffer against its will. Giving oneself up is perhaps less catastrophic than suffering the end of my life passively – simply watching how death puts an end to me, to my self, my existence.

Heidegger briefly considers death as the 'measureless impossibility of existence', as that endpoint where Dasein ceases to exist, only in order quickly to turn towards the investigation of being. In this turn towards being, death is experienced as a *measure-providing* possibility of existence. In what sense is it possible to speak of a catastrophe in this context? Does death subvert being? Where does death leave being after it brings about its downfall?

Dasein lives 'proximally and for the most part' in the everyday, as Heidegger's famous thesis has it. Self-forgetful or oblivious of self, it lives in the moment. Under conditions of everydayness, Dasein takes the familiar patterns of perception and activities of the 'they' [*das Man*] as the basis for orientation. Death is a catastrophe to the extent that it pulls Dasein out of the certainty of its familiar world, that it leads to the 'collapse' of this world.[22] This world catastrophe puts Dasein in a 'mood of uncanniness'.[23] What is uncanny is thus not the end of being, not the nothingness that follows after, but being itself in its unfamiliar nakedness.

However, because *I* do not collapse, the collapse of the world is not a complete catastrophe. Rather, the 'naked uncanniness' of being throws Dasein upon itself.[24] When the everyday world – where Dasein proximally and for the most part lives, oblivious of self and for the moment – sinks away, an intense self awakes. Dasein takes hold of itself. Death does not put Dasein into a state of radical passivity. Rather, it represents a departure or a turning point. In the face of death, Dasein awakens to that authentic existence that, in contrast to the inauthentic existence of the 'they', is the existence of an intense self. Death calls Dasein into 'resoluteness towards itself'.[25] It calls, shakes up, Dasein into wakefulness. It 'discloses to Dasein its *ownmost* potentiality-for-Being'.[26] Dasein is thus re-*minded* of *itself*, of its *I-am*.[27]

> At my age even I
>   am timid when faced with a
>   scarecrow in the field
>   – Issa

Heidegger's 'Being-Towards-Death' is heroic. According to Heidegger, anxiety in the face of death as a passing away is a weak mood. By contrast, an attitude that looks death in the eye, lingers on death, on the collapse of the everyday world, is heroic. This heroic being-towards-death is the 'magical power' that helps Dasein to achieve its ownmost being. In another way, it helps to turn the negative into being. What is required is a heroic resoluteness that comes to terms with anxiety. 'Anxiety in the face of death' is not anxiety about the end of being but anxiety about being as such, the being I have to take upon myself in my individuation.

In being-towards-death, towards 'my death', an intense 'I am' stirs:

> With death, which at its time is only my dying, my ownmost being stands before me, is imminent: I stand before my can-be at every moment. The being that I will be in the 'last' of my Dasein, that I can be at any moment, this possibility is that of my ownmost 'I am', which means that I will be my ownmost I. I myself am this possibility, where death is my death.[28]

Dasein reacts to the possibility of 'giving itself up' – which would actually be a loss of self, an end to the self that must be passively endured – with a heroic 'resoluteness towards itself'.[29] Thus, death does not put an end to what is *mine*. Instead, as *my* death, it calls forth an intense *I am*. I am dying therefore means: *I am*. A heroic being-towards-death turns death into a being whose positive content is called 'I am'.

> still not a butterfly
>> as autumn deepens:
>>> a rape-worm
>>>> – Bashō[30]

For Heidegger, death certainly does not promise infinity in the Platonic sense. 'Dasein' does not flee from the body, the place of finitude, in order to approach infinity. Nor would Heidegger wish to be associated with Fichte's jubilant 'Thus do I live, thus am I, and thus am I unchangeable, firm, and completed for all Eternity.'[31] But a heroism or desire arises again. The intense 'I am' that is evoked in the face of death is, after all, ultimately a heroic turn against human finitude, for death puts an end to the 'I am'. A relationship to death that remained aware of finitude, by contrast, would be a being-towards-death in which the grasp of the I relaxed.

In Zen Buddhism, death is not a catastrophe or a scandal, but nor does it set in motion a labour of mourning that *works* compulsively against finitude. It does not involve an economy of mourning that aims to convert 'nothingness' into 'being'. Rather, in the face of death Zen Buddhism cultivates an attitude of letting go [*Gelassenheit*] that is free of heroism and desire, that keeps pace with finitude, so to speak, instead of working against it.

From his early years, Dōgen was forced to confront death and impermanence. One of his biographers writes:

At the loss of his beloved mother at the age of seven his grief was profound. As he saw the incense ascending in the

Takao temple he recognized the arising and the decay – the transitoriness – of all things. Thereby the desire for enlightenment was awakened in his heart.[32]

This enlightenment, however, would not have consisted in an overcoming of impermanence. Shortly before his death, Dōgen wrote:

> To what indeed shall I liken
> The world and the life of man?
> Ah, the shadow of the moon,
> When it touches in the drop of dew
> The beak of the waterfowl.[33]

These words express the frailty, impermanence and fleetingness of things in a calmly resonant way; the words do not point to what is other. Without heroism, without desire, Dōgen dwells with the transient things. He does not attempt to look beyond impermanence. The following words from Issa express a similar mood and spirit:

> In no moment of my life did the thought of frailty and impermanence leave me; I realized that all things in the world are short lived and fade away as fast as a lightning flash. I wandered around until my hair became as white as winter frost.[34]

Issa wanders through impermanence while keeping pace with the things that are happening. He stays with the transient immanent world instead of elevating himself above it. He is friendly towards it. He joins in the impermanence; he lets *himself* pass away too. In this unique letting go [*Gelassenheit*], finitude is illuminated from within itself. Finitude begins to shine, without the brilliance of infinity or the semblance of eternity. When we listen closely to Issa's words, we can hear a mourning that approaches a kind of serenity. We are faced with a mourning that is liberated into serenity, that has a clearing towards the open. This serenity differs from a cheerfulness that does not know mourning.

> One should be trustful
> blossoms whither – fade away
> each in its own way
> – Issa

Dōgen writes: 'In order to depart from egocentric self, seeing impermanence is the primary necessity.'[35] What Dōgen has in mind is a particular way of experiencing impermanence: it is not the perception of impermanence as such that leads to selflessness. When we resist impermanence, the self intensifies. I expand *myself*; I allow the I to grow against death, the death that is *my* death and that ends the I. When we 'awaken to impermanence' and let ourselves pass away, a different perception of mortality arises.[36]

When I give death to myself, when I empty myself out, death is no longer *my* death. It no longer has anything dramatic about it. I am no longer tied to the death that is *my* death. There awakens in me an attitude of letting go, a freedom towards death. The basis of Heidegger's 'impassioned freedom towards death' is an altogether different mental attitude.[37] It is accompanied by an intense 'I am', by a heroic resoluteness to *oneself*. Zen Buddhism's freedom towards death, by contrast, originates in a kind of *I-am-not*. It bids farewell not only to the egotistic self but also to I-like and soul-like inwardness. The awakening to impermanence de-internalizes the I. Death becomes not an outstanding possibility of being oneself but a unique possibility of awakening to selflessness, of not being an *I*.

Case forty-one of the *Bi-yan-lu* says: 'How is it when one who has died the great death returns to life?'[38] The 'great death' does not end life. The death that occurs at the end of life is a 'small' death. Of course, only a human being is capable of the 'great death'. A great death means taking away the risk that *oneself* will die, but it does not undo the self. Rather, it clears it into the open. The self empties itself out by filling itself with a world-like vastness. This unique kind of death leads to the emergence of a self that is filled with vastness, a selfless self.

For Hegel, death involves the self's circumference, as it were, expanding into generality. It raises the inwardness of the individual to the level of the inwardness of the general. The fundamental characteristic of Hegel's spirit is internalization. The fundamental movement of the 'great death', by contrast, is de-internalization. The all-encompassing unity into which the self suspends *itself* is therefore free of subjective inwardness. It is *empty* in itself. It is neither substance nor subject. The 'great death' is thus more catastrophic than the dialectical death because it negates all subject-hood or I-hood.

Despite a certain similarity, the 'great death' differs from the *mors mystica*. Although Eckhart avers that the soul loses 'all her desire' in death,[39] the soul's desire returns at a higher level. 'Dying in God' is animated by a striving for infinity.[40] In 'divine death',[41] the soul fuses fully with God, and 'nothing dies'.[42] Eckhart's example of the nobleness of being indirectly suggests that striving is part of its character: 'When caterpillars drop off a tree, they crawl up a wall to preserve their being, so noble is being.'[43] In dying in God, nothing is meant to be lost. It is accompanied by a deep trust in the divine economy: 'nature never breaks anything without giving something better. . . . If this is nature's way, how much more is it God's: He never destroys without giving something better.'[44] And: 'We advocate dying in God so that He may place us in a being which is better than life.'[45] 'Dying in God' takes place out of 'love' of God, but this 'love' entangles the lover in narcissism. Death does not kill inwardness itself. Rather, inwardness is raised to, or reflected into, the infinite inwardness of that 'Godhead' that 'hovers in itself', which 'lives as no one other than itself'.[46]

In contrast to the *mors mystica*, the great death of Zen Buddhism is a phenomenon of immanence, an immanent turning point. The impermanent world is not transcended towards infinity. You do not move *somewhere else*. Rather, you immerse yourself in impermanence. The forty-third case of the *Bi-yan-lu* illustrates this unique turn:

> A monk asked Dongshan, 'When cold and heat come, how can we avoid them?' . . . Dongshan said, 'Why not go where there is no cold or heat?' . . . The monk said, 'Where is there no cold or heat?' . . . Dongshan said, 'When it's cold, it chills you thoroughly; when it's hot, it heats you thoroughly.'[47]
>
> . . .
>
> Also Caoshan asked a monk, 'When it's so hot, where will you go to avoid it?' The monk said, 'I'll avoid it in a boiling cauldron, in the coals of a furnace.' Caoshan said, 'How can it be avoided in a boiling cauldron or in coals of a furnace?' The monk said, 'Sufferings cannot reach there.'[48]

You immerse yourself in the heat or cold instead of labouring against it; then there is *no one* to *suffer* it.

Case fifty-five of the *Bi-yan-lu* relates an anecdote about life and death:

> Daowu and Jianyuan went to make a condolence call. Jianyuan hit the coffin and said, 'Alive or dead?' . . . Daowu said, 'I won't say alive, and I won't say dead.' . . . Jianyuan

said, 'Why won't you say?' ... Daowu said, 'I won't say, I won't say.' On the way back ... Jianyuan said, 'Tell me right away, or I'll hit you.' ... Daowu said, 'You may hit me, but I won't say.' ... Jianyuan then hit him. ... Later Daowu passed on. Jianyuan went to Shishuang and told him this story. ... Shishuang said, 'I won't say, I won't say.' ... At these words Jianyuan had an insight.[49]

What is the reason for Master Daowu's stubborn refusal to say anything? What kind of saying shines through his not-saying? What insight does Jianyuan suddenly arrive at in response to Daowu's silence? Daowu refrains from judgement, as though judgement produces separations and contradictions that suspend the possibility that the beginning of the fifty-fifth case describes: 'Secure in complete reality, one obtains realization right there.'[50] By refraining from judgement, Master Daowu stays in the realm of in-difference, *prior to* any distinction between life and death.

Before the separation of 'life' and 'death', one lives *fully*. Before the separation of 'life' and 'death', one dies *fully*. *Care* originates from their distinction, which is also inherent in the act of judgement. One should not look beyond 'life' in order to constitute it as the wholly other of 'death': 'It is the same, for example, with winter and spring. We do not think that winter becomes spring, and we do not say that spring becomes summer.'[51] This mental attitude goes along with a unique experience of time. One dwells fully in the present. This fulfilled present of letting go is not *scattered* into a before and after. It does not look beyond itself; rather, it rests in itself. This time of letting go [*gelassene Zeit*] leaves behind the time of care. The satisfied present also differs from the 'moment' that moves out of or protrudes from the rest of time as a special point in time. It is an *ordinary* time. It lacks any intensity.

81

In the commentary to the verse of case forty-one, Yuan-wu quotes a Zen saying: 'Utterly kill the dead, and then you will see the living; enliven the dead and you will see the dead.'[52] Someone who is alive remains dead as long as 'death' has not been killed, that is, as long as he opposes 'death' to 'life'. Only once you have fully killed 'death' are you fully alive; that is, you live fully by not staring at 'death' as the other of life. Whether someone is *fully alive* is not a matter of his life being 'eternal' or 'immortal'. Rather, it is about being *fully mortal*.

Death is no longer a catastrophe because the *katastrophe* of the great death already lies behind you. *No one* dies. The Zen Buddhist transformation of death takes place without the labour of mourning. It does not turn the finite into the infinite. It does not labour against mortality. Rather, it turns death inwards. *You die while dying.* This unique kind of death is another way of escaping catastrophe.

Friendliness

The servant, quite dumb:
he shovels the neighbour's snow,
too.

– Issa

I pointed out before that emptiness must be understood as a *medium of friendliness*. In the field of emptiness, there are no strict demarcations. Nothing remains isolated in itself or within itself. Things nestle up to one another, reflect each other. Emptiness de-*internalizes* the I into a *rei amicae* that opens up like a guest house. Human being-with-one-another can also be understood in these terms.

Case sixty-eight of the *Bi-yan-lu* expresses a unique inter-personal relation to language: 'Yangshan (Hui-dji) asked Sansheng (Hui-jan): What is your name, then? Sansheng said: Hui-dji. Yangshan said: But I am Hui-dji! Sansheng said: Then my name is Hui-jan. Yangshan laughed mightily: ha, ha, ha!'[1] Huiran calls himself by the other's name, thereby toppling over his own name, so to speak. By thus pushing *himself*, or pushing away himself, into the field of emptiness, he turns *himself* into a *no one*. He suspends *himself* in that emptiness where there is no *difference* between the I and the other.

In the second step of the dialogue, each of the interlocutors returns to his proper name, or to *himself*. I have mentioned several times that emptiness is not a denial of the proper but an affirmation of it. What it denies is only the substance-like insistence on oneself. The first step of the conversation is thus a 'no' that kills the self. Yangshan and Sansheng ruin each other [*richten einander zugrunde*] – that is, they suspend each other into emptiness.[2] The second step, a 'yes', *animates* the self again. This simultaneous 'no' and 'yes' creates an open, friendly self. The laughter is elicited by the relaxation that liberates the self from its rigidity. Yangshan laughs beyond himself, laughs *himself* away, liberates himself into that in-difference that is the place of *original friendliness*.

The verse of the sixty-eighth case of the *Bi-yan-lu* expresses the double movement of 'no' and 'yes':

Both take in, both let go – how do you find the source?
. . .
To ride a tiger always requires absolute competence.
. . .
His laughter ended, I don't know where he's gone;
. . .
It is only fitting to stir forever the wind of lament.[3]

The taking in or killing represents an ex-*propriating* 'no'. Both participants in the conversation ex-*propriate* themselves, give each other their death and thereby liberate themselves into that emptiness in which there is neither an 'I' nor a 'thou'. The 'no' suspends all differences. The letting go [*Lösen*], by contrast, represents the movement of the 'yes', that is, the letting live or animating that again permits the face to face of 'I' and 'thou', or the proper figure of each. The verse talks of laughter; laughter, this pure wind, stirs 'the wind of lament' – 'forever'. This serene laughter breezes across from emptiness, the medium of friendliness. It is proper to those who have died the 'great death', who no longer labour in mourning.

The Zen saying 'Neither host nor guest. Host and guest, obviously' expresses the same movement.[4] Hospitality has its origin in that place where there are no differences or rigid distinctions between host and guest, where the host is not at home in his place but is rather himself a guest. That kind of hospitality is altogether different from the 'generosity' through which a host pleases *himself*. 'Neither host nor guest' suspends exactly this *himself*. The guest house of original friendliness is the possession of *no one*.

Original friendliness is clearly opposed to the interpersonal constellation between two totalities as described by Hegel, in which, instead of emptying themselves out, each side attempts to posit itself as an absolute self. Here, the I seeks to be registered and recognized in the consciousness of the other as an I that totally excludes the other. Only through the exclusion of the other can the I be a true totality. Each I posits as absolute what is proper to it. The merest questioning of my property becomes the concern of the totality of my self:

> The injuring of any one of his single aspects is therefore infinite, it is an absolute offense, and offense against his integrity, an offense to his honor; and the collision about any single point is a struggle for the whole.[5]

Assigning absolute value to one's own is quite opposed to the generosity that expresses original friendliness, which rests on selflessness and propertyless being.

85

The battle between two totalities results from the fact that the other also wants to posit himself as an exclusive totality in my consciousness. The two parties therefore face each other as absolute opponents. This absolute opposition could be called *original hostility*. Here, friendly words are impossible. Insult and injury rule the being-towards-the-other: 'Hence they must injure one another. The fact that each posits himself as exclusive totality in the singularity of his existence must become actual; the offense is necessary.'[6] In order to appear to the other as an exclusive totality, and be recognized by the other as such a totality, I have to insult, injure and negate the other. In my desire to posit myself as the exclusive totality, I must seek the death of the other. In doing so, however, I expose myself to the danger of death. I not only risk injury (Hegel speaks of a 'wound') but put my whole existence at stake. But the one who, out of fear of death, does not risk his own life 'becomes the slave of the other'.[7] The battle between two totalities is a battle over life and death:

> If he stops short of death in the other's case, and suspends the conflict before putting him to death, then neither has he proved himself as totality nor has he come to cognizance of the other as such.[8]

The heroic resolution to face death goes along with a resolution to achieve a self. Original hostility is the interpersonal expression of this heroic being-towards-death. In contrast to the 'great death' of Zen Buddhism, in which one awakens to selflessness, the Hegelian risk of death is tied to that intense consciousness of self that completely excludes the other. The heroic I does not smile.

The old man in the final picture in *The Ox and His Herdsman*, whose cheeks are filled with laughter, is perhaps a visual representation of original friendliness. His laughter shakes any separation or delimitation at its foundations: 'If he flashes the iron staff as quickly as the wind – / Amply and wide suddenly open doors and gates.'[9] Friendliness and generosity fill his heart:

> He mixes with the light and the dust with an open and generous heart. What can one call him? An independent, open-hearted and really human being? A fool? A saint? He is the 'holy fool'.
>
> He hides nothing. Master Hui-tang once went with the layman Huang-shan-gu into the mountains. A fragrant smell suddenly reached them. Hui-tang asked, 'Can you smell the perfume of the mignonettes?' When Huang-shan-gu replied that he could, Hui-tang told him, 'I have nothing to hide from you.' Huang-shan-gu was awakened in a flash.[10]

Hui-tang's remark 'I have nothing to hide from you' is a *friendly* one. It comes from an 'open and generous heart'. The perfume of the mignonettes de-*internalizes* Hui-tang, or fills his emptied-*out* heart. Original friendliness is not something that is exchanged between persons; it is not a case of 'someone' being friendly towards 'someone'. Rather, one should say: *no one* is friendly. Original friendliness is not something expressed by a person. It is a gesture of emptiness.

Original friendliness differs from the kind of communicative friendliness through which people present themselves to one another in a good light. In communicative friendliness, what counts as 'friendly' are the words that allow the others an unhindered self-presentation. Communicative friendliness focuses on the self. Original friendliness, by contrast, rests on selflessness. It must also be distinguished from the friendliness through which one keeps one's distance from the other in order to hide or protect one's own inner life. Unlike this protective friendliness, original friendliness derives from an unlimited openness.

Original friendliness and Nietzsche's aristocratic friendliness have entirely different origins. Nietzsche's *Daybreak* contains a notable aphorism:

> *A different kind of neighbour-love.* – Behaviour that is excited, noisy, inconsistent, nervous constitutes the antithesis of *great passion*: the latter, dwelling within like a dark fire [*düstere Gluth* = dark glow] and there assembling all that is hot and ardent, leaves a man looking outwardly cold and indifferent and impresses upon his features a certain impassivity. Such men are, to be sure, occasionally capable of *neighbour-love* – but it is a kind different from that of the sociable and anxious to please: it is a gentle, reflective, relaxed friendliness; it is as though they were gazing out of the windows of their castle, which is their fortress and for that reason also their prison – to gaze into what is strange and free, into *what is different*, does them so much good![11]

This aristocratic friendliness implies a crowded, overflowing inner life that remains a 'fortress' separated from the outside. It is a friendliness of 'windows' behind which inwardness glows; it is the friendliness of windowed monads. It does not go beyond the nobleness of that gentle, reflective gaze that meets the other while keeping a distance. The 'castle' or 'fortress' lacks original openness. Its poise [*Gelassenheit*] resembles self-complacency. The 'impassivity' is opposed to the permeability of original friendliness, in which the distinction between inner and outer is suspended. Those who are originally friendly do not need a 'window' in order to move outside of themselves, because they do not live in a house or castle. They have no inwardness. They do not have an interior from which they may sometimes break out or wish to break out, for they live *outside*, or rather *nowhere*. Original friendliness derives not from the fullness of inwardness, or of the self, but from *emptiness*. It is without passion, in-different, like drifting clouds. It has no inner 'glow'. Original friendliness further differs from the *gentillesse* that points towards aristocratic 'noblesse'. It is *common* rather than belonging to *nobility* or *gentility*.

Original friendliness is *older* than the good, *older* than any moral law. It may be understood as a ground-providing ethical force: 'No one can render the free play of his life intellectually comprehensible; it is beyond laws or rules. It is actually from this freely playing life that all moral laws and religious rules spring in the first place.'[12]

> Deep autumn –
> my neighbor,
>   how does he live, I wonder?
>   – Bashō[13]

Mettā is a fundamental concept of Buddhist 'ethics'. It means, roughly, benevolence or friendliness. *Mettā* is derived from *mitra*, meaning 'friend'. Original friendliness, however, cannot be comprehended from the perspective of an economy of friendship that circles around the self. Aristotle, for example, derives the relation of friendship from the relation to self. The virtuous man 'is related to his friend as to himself'. The friend is thus 'another self [*allos auto*]',[14] and 'the extreme of friendship is likened to one's love for oneself'.[15] In the *Eudemian Ethics*, Aristotle writes:

> Therefore the perceiving of one's friend must in a way be the perceiving of oneself and in a way the knowing of oneself. Consequently, even enjoying the vulgar things and living together with one's friend is understandably pleasant – for

there is, as just mentioned, always perception of one's own self at the same time.[16]

In this way, friendship is a mirroring relation between *oneself* and the other. In our friends, we perceive *ourselves*. In the other, we enjoy *ourselves*. The essence of the friend is therefore that he is *my* friend. He is a representation of the I. By contrast, the emptiness from which original friendliness flows de-*mirrors* that self-based relationship with the other by de-*internalizing* and *emptying* out the I.

Nor does a friendship of fusion suspend inwardness, for here inwardness is restored at the level of the *we*. Montaigne, for example, says of the loss of a friend:

> Since the day when I lost him, I have dragged out but a languishing existence, and even such pleasures as come to me, far from consoling me, redouble my grief for his loss. We were equal partners in everything, and I seem to be robbing him of his share.

> 'I have resolved to enjoy no pleasures, while he is not here to share them with me.'

> I had grown so accustomed to be his second self in everything that now I seem to be no more than half a man.[17]

For Montaigne, a friend is a 'second self'. Such a friendship of fusion doubles the I. The 'we' is an 'I in twos'. The individuals are no longer separate, but they are still deeply entangled in inwardness. In order to get to original friendship, it is necessary to cut all ties with inwardness. The other towards whom original friendliness is directed is a *third* figure.

For Aristotle, equality and the exchange of equivalents are fundamental to friendship: 'thus a friend comes to be when, being loved, he loves back and neither of them fails in any way to notice the fact'.[18] Accordingly, it is not possible to be friends with something that does not have a soul, or an animal, because here there is no possibility of reciprocity.[19] The 'beginnings and springs of friendship' are in the household.[20] The relationship between parents and their children, whom parents love as 'a sort of other selves', would be an archetype for friendship.[21] Strangers are those who are outside the household. It is 'nobler to do well by friends than by strangers'.[22] The law of the household (*oikos*) dominates the Greek idea of friendship. *Oikeios* means 'belonging to the family or kinship' as well as 'friendly' or 'befriended'. The Greek word for *relatives* is the same as the superlative of 'friend'. Dōgen, by contrast, says:

> Have compassion for living beings without distinguishing between the intimate and the unrelated and maintain an attitude of saving all equally. Never think of your own profit in terms of worldly or supraworldly benefit. Even though you are neither known nor appreciated, just do good for others according to your own heart and do not show others that you have such a spirit.[23]

In many ways, original friendliness is opposed to the Aristotelian idea of friendship. To begin with, its origin is not the 'household'. Someone who exhibits original friendliness dwells nowhere. He does not take as his point of orientation the house (*oikos*), which is the place of *proper*-ty and possession, or the place of inwardness. He transcends everything to do with *house*keeping, that is, any economy based on exchange or equivalence. He is the de-*internalized* and dis-*possessed* friend of all beings. He is friendly not only towards other human beings but towards all beings.

The Christian love for one's enemy is not free of the economic either. The demand that one should give without seeking anything in return goes along with a sacred economy. What is expected is a divine reward:

> And if ye lend *to them* of whom ye hope to receive, what thank have ye? for sinners also lend to sinners, to receive as much again.

> But love ye your enemies, and do good, and lend, hoping for nothing again; and your reward shall be great . . .

> Give, and it shall be given unto you; good measure, pressed down, and shaken together, and running over, shall men give into your bosom. For with the same measure that ye mete withal it shall be measured to you again.[24]

In Zen Buddhism, by contrast, there is no divine authority to restore the economic balance on a higher level. One gives and forgives without entering into any economic calculation. There is no one who practises *house*keeping.

The compassion that arises out of original friendliness cannot be understood in terms of what is commonly called 'sympathy'. For one thing, it is directed not at fellow human beings alone but at all beings. For another, it is not the result of identifying or 'empathizing' with others. The compassion of friendliness does not know the I that, by identifying with others, shares in their suffering or joy. If all 'feelings' necessarily belonged to a subject then compassion could not be called a 'feeling'. Compassion is not a subjective feeling or inclination. It is not *my* feeling. *No one* feels. Compassion is something that *happens* to you. *It* is friendly:

> He [the Zen Buddhist] is joyful and suffers not as if it were 'he' who is joyful or suffering. He feels the same about it

as when breathing: it is not 'he' who is breathing, as if the breathing depended on him and his consent, but he is being breathed and, if anything, plays the part of a conscious observer.[25]

The friendly *with* is owed to that emptiness from which the distinction between the I and what is other has been removed. It does not allow for the self that, in showing compassion, likes *itself*: 'Compassion . . . must not in the least favour complacency.'[26] The friendly *with* is rooted in an original in-difference, an attitude that affords everything equal *validity* [Gleich-*Gültigkeit*].[27] It is free of hate and love, free of affection and dislike.

According to Schopenhauer, compassion arises wherever one moves beyond the *principium individuationis*, through which I posit my 'will-to-live' as absolutely prior to others. If this happens, however, it does not mean that the 'will-to-live' itself is suspended. The will-to-live is the in-itself of the man-ifest world; it 'constitutes the inner nature of everything, and lives in all'.[28] Rather, moving beyond the *principium individu-ationis* is the moment when one recognizes that the in-itself of one's own phenomenon, namely the will-to-live, is also that of all others. Once the grip of the *principium individuationis* is loosened, a person tries to restore the balance between himself and others, 'denies himself pleasures, undergoes pri-vations, in order to alleviate another's suffering. He perceives that the distinction between himself and others, which to the wicked man is so great a gulf, belongs only to a fleeting, deceptive phenomenon.'[29]

Schopenhauer's ethics of compassion is located beyond the moral 'ought' and normative ethics. But unlike Zen Buddhism, Schopenhauer's ethics of compassion still involves the rule of the will over the relation to the other. When I am compassionate, the 'other person becomes *the ultimate object* of my will'.[30] I *want* the weal of the other because he is 'myself once more'.[31] Someone who is compassionate recognizes 'himself, his will' in the one who is suffering.[32] Schopenhauer's ethics of compassion remains attached to the figure of the self. It therefore needs to solve the problem of the identification between self and other. For compassion requires that 'I must in some way or other *be identified with him*; that is, the *difference* between myself and him, which is the precise *raison d'être* of my Egoism, must be removed, at least to a certain extent'.[33] According to Schopenhauer, this identification takes place by way of a mental picture [*Vorstellung*]:

> Now, since I do not live *in his skin*, there remains only the *knowledge*, that is, the mental picture, I have of him, as the possible means whereby I can so far identify myself with him, that my action declares the difference to be practically effaced.[34]

The difference between ourselves and the other is, however, only removed 'to a certain extent':

> The conviction never leaves us for a moment that *he* is the sufferer, not *we*; and it is precisely *in his* person, not in ours, that we feel the distress which afflicts us. We suffer *with* him, and therefore *in* him; we feel his trouble as *his*, and are not under the delusion that it is ours.[35]

As is well known, Martin Buber locates the dialogical relation between I and Thou in a 'realm of "between"', on that 'narrow ridge', that is, 'on the far side of the subjective, on this side of the objective'.[36] The relation 'does not take place in each of the participants or in a neutral world which includes the two and all other things; but it takes place *between* them in the

94

most precise sense'.[37] This is an interesting approach insofar as it places the inter-human process outside of the *inwardness* of subjects that have been separated from each other. The 'between' in which the relation between individuals takes place is *older* than them, so to speak. It denotes a relation that cannot be turned into a substance and that precedes what it relates.

The emptiness of Zen Buddhism differs from Buber's 'between' in several ways. It is the place of in-difference, of the neither-I-nor-Thou. The 'between', by contrast, is not as empty or open as the emptiness. It is enclosed from both *ends*, from where the I and Thou have their fixed positions. The dialogical relation, or 'meeting',[38] may take place outside of the inwardness of the individual subjects, but the 'between' itself condenses into a space of inwardness. It assumes the closed nature and intimacy of an interior. One might even say: the 'between' has a *soul*. The conversation between Yangshan and Sansheng, by contrast, does not develop an intimate dialogue. In particular, the loud 'laughter' punctures any intimacy, any inwardness of a 'between'.

Buber's examples of the dialogical relation clearly illustrate the intimacy and closed nature of this dyadic relation:

> In the deadly crush of an air-raid shelter the glances of two strangers suddenly meet for a second in astonishing and unrelated mutuality; when the All Clear sounds it is forgotten; and yet it did happen, in a realm which existed only for that moment. In the darkened opera-house there can be established between two of the audience, who do not know one another, and who are listening in the same purity and with the same intensity to the music of Mozart, a relation which is scarcely perceptible and yet is one of elemental dialogue, and which has long vanished when the lights blaze up again.[39]

At the moment of their dialogical meeting, the two individuals involved stand out from the rest; they move into the interior of the dialogue, or the 'between'. The Thou has 'no neighbour'.[40] Buber frequently stresses the exclusiveness of the dialogical relation: 'Every real relation with a being or life in the world is exclusive. Its Thou is freed, steps forth, is single, and confronts you. It fills the heavens. This does not mean that nothing else exists; but all else lives in *its* light.'[41] The exclusiveness of the Thou, the fact that it has no neighbours, gives the 'between' a deep inwardness. Original friendliness, devoid of inwardness, is not familiar with the Thou.

According to Buber, it is 'the exalted melancholy of our fate, that every Thou in our world must become an It':[42]

> The human being who was even now single and unconditioned, not something lying to hand, only present, not able to be experienced, only able to be fulfilled, has now become again a *He* or a *She*, a sum of qualities, a given quantity with a certain shape.[43]

The It is a something, an object to be appropriated. Unlike the Thou-I, the It-I is incapable of forming a relation, because its behaviour towards the world is exclusively one of appropriation:

> It is said that man experiences his world. What does that mean?
>
> Man travels over the surface of things and experiences them. He extracts knowledge about their constitution from them: he wins an experience from them. He experiences what belongs to the things.
>
> But the world is not presented to man by experiences alone. These present him only with a world composed of It and He and She and It again.

I experience something. . . .

As experience, the world belongs to the primary word I-It.

The primary word I-Thou establishes the world of relation.[44]

The individual Thou is finite. After the brief moment of meeting, it becomes It again. But the Thou remains fixed in God, that is, in that 'eternal *Thou*' that, by virtue of its very nature, cannot become an It.[45]

Buber's dialogical thinking ends in a theology. All invocations of the Thou circle around the 'eternal Thou'. They are ultimately invocations of God, and 'every particular *Thou* is a glimpse through to the eternal *Thou*':[46]

> In every sphere in its own way, through each process of becoming that is present to us, we look out toward the fringe of the eternal *Thou*; in each we are aware of a breath from the eternal *Thou*; in each *Thou* we address the eternal *Thou*.[47]

As I have mentioned, every dialogical relation is exclusive, so the lines of relation, if they could be extended at all, would need to run in parallel without touching each other. But Buber *bundles* the dialogical lines together and has them run towards a centre: 'The extended lines of relations meet in the eternal *Thou*.'[48] The 'context' of the Thou world 'is in the Centre, where the extended lines of relations meet – in the *eternal* Thou'.[49] By means of this circular figure, Buber attributes a further inwardness to the dialogical 'between'. An internalizing centring takes place. The 'between', which is already gathered in itself, also *gathers itself* into the divine centre. This plural inwardness again illustrates the difference between the dialogical 'between' and the Zen Buddhist emptiness whose fundamental trait is de-internalization. The invocations of the Thou circle around God, around 'the

Lord of the Voice'.[50] The voices that are directed exclusively at a Thou are further internalized within the voice of God. Community is based not on a *neighbourly conversation with each other* but on those 'radiuses' that run towards the divine centre: 'It is not the periphery, the community, that comes first, but the radii, the common quality of relation with the Centre. This alone guarantees the authentic existence of the community.'[51] Original friendliness, which comes out of emptiness, lacks precisely this 'centre', which also means that it has no peripheries or radiuses. Original friendliness articulates a 'being-with' without any centre or centripetal force.

As a word of love and affirmation, Buber's 'Thou' is said with great emphasis.[52] Profound emotion or sublimity is the fundamental mood that *determines* the dialogical relation.[53] It would not be right to call 'Thou' a *friendly* word. Original friendliness lacks emphatic intensity, inwardness and intimacy, for it does not exclude. The friendly word opens up the dialogical interior, sounds out across 'I' and 'Thou'. It is in many respects in-different. It is this in-difference that takes inwardness away from it and makes it *more common, more open*, than the word 'love', which is directed at the Thou.

In *I and Thou*, Buber accuses Buddhism of being incapable of entering into a 'relation'; Buddhism, he says, means the 'extinction of the ability to say Thou'.[54] To Buddha, he says, the 'simple confrontation of being with being is alien'.[55] According to Buber, Buddhism, like 'all doctrine of absorption', lapses into the 'colossal illusion of the human spirit that is bent back on itself'. Under this illusion, spirit forfeits any sense of relation: 'the spirit that is bent back on itself is compelled to drag into man that which is not man, it is compelled to make the world and God into functions of the soul'.[56]

a spring unseen:
> on the back of a mirror,
> plum blossoms
> – Bashō[57]

There are several questionable aspects of Buber's interpretation of Buddhism. First of all, Buddhism does not know this human inwardness, this isolated cell of pure 'subject' that is 'bent back on itself' – an inwardness into which everything must be internalized and turned 'into functions of the soul'. On the contrary, in Buddhism, spirit is to be de-internalized. Open, friendly spirit is always already *outside*. The dialogical relation, by contrast, assumes an inwardness of the 'I', from which is issued an appeal to a 'Thou' that is separated from it. Original friendliness does not require such an appeal because it is awakened by the unique *It* of in-difference, which, however, needs to be distinguished from Buber's It-world. The It of in-difference allows for a relation that is a being-with without inwardness and desire:

> The mortar, too, is Issa!
> – Issa[58]

Buddhist chronicles tell of the event when Shakyamuni passed on the 'light' to his disciple Kāśyapa. Dōgen also frequently refers to this special event:

> Before an assembly of millions on Vulture Peak, the World-honored One picks up an *uḍumbara*[59] flower and winks. Thereupon the face of Mahākāśyapa breaks into a smile. The World-honored One says, 'I possess the right Dharma-eye treasury and the fine mind of nirvana; I transmit them to Mahākāśyapa.'[60]

Mahākāśyapa's smile is certainly not a 'sign' of the fact that he has understood Shakyamuni's 'sign'. Nothing here is 'interpreted'. No 'signs' are exchanged. Dōgen comments on the picking and holding up of the flower as follows:

> In general, the mountains, rivers, and the earth; the sun and moon, the wind and rain; people, animals, grass, and trees – the miscellaneous things of the present displaying themselves here and there – are just the twirling of the *uḍumbara* flower. Living-and-dying and going-and-coming are also a miscellany of flowers and the brightness of flowers.[61]

The flower that is being held up *is* the manifold world; it is the life and death, the coming and going, of beings. The smile does not 'point' to anything. Rather, it is the *process of a unique transformation* in which Kāśyapa becomes the flower:

> 'A wink' describes the moment in which, while [the Buddha] sat under the [*bodhi*] tree, the bright star took the place of his eyes. In this moment 'the face of Mahākāśyapa breaks into a smile'. The face has broken already, and its place has been taken by the face of twirling flowers.[62]

Kāśyapa's smiling face *is* the world. It *is* life and death, coming and going. It *is* the vis-*age* [*Ge*-Sicht] of each presently dwelling thing. This *emptied*-out, de-*internalized*, selfless flower-face, which *breathes*, receives or reflects mountains and rivers, earth, sun and moon, wind and rain, human beings, animals, grass and trees, could be described as the place of original friendliness. The *original smile*, this deep expression of friendliness, is awakened when the face breaks out of its rigidity, becomes *bound*-less, and is transformed, as if it were the *face of no one*.

NOTES

Preface

1 *Mahā* means 'large'; *yāna* means 'vehicle'. Thus, the literal translation of Mahāyāna is 'large vehicle'. Buddhism is a path to salvation that provides a 'vehicle' that is meant to lead living creatures out of their painful existence. The teaching of Buddha therefore does not offer a 'truth' but a 'vehicle', a 'means' that would become superfluous once the goal has been reached. That makes Buddhist discourse free of the compulsion to truth that dominates Christian discourse. As opposed to Hīnayāna Buddhism ('small vehicle'), which aims at self-perfection, Mahāyāna Buddhism strives for the salvation of all living creatures. Therefore, the Bodhisattva, despite having reached complete enlightenment, lives among the suffering creatures in order to lead them to salvation.

2 It is said that he came to China as the twenty-eighth Indian patriarch in order to found the Chinese line of the Zen tradition.

3 Heinrich Dumoulin, *A History of Zen Buddhism*, New York: Pantheon, 1963, p. 87.

4 See *The Blue Cliff Record* (*Bi-yan-lu*), compiled by Ch'ung-hsien and commented upon by K'o-ch'in, trans. Thomas Cleary, Berkeley: Numata Center for Buddhist Translation and Research, 1998: 'Elder Ding asked Linji, "What is the meaning of Buddhism?" Linji got off his seat, grabbed Ding, slapped him, then pushed him away. Ding stood there motionless. A monk standing by said, "Elder Ding, why don't you bow?" Just as Ding bowed, he suddenly was greatly enlightened' (pp. 171f.).

5 Transl. note: In many cases, there are several, often very different, English translations of a haiku. I have selected the ones that are closest to the German translations. In a few instances I have given, in footnotes, alternative translations that follow the German versions more literally. Where no reference is given, the translations are mine.

A Religion without God

1 Georg Wilhelm Friedrich Hegel, *Lectures on the Philosophy of Religion*, vol. 1, London: Kegan Paul, 1895, p. 19.

2 Georg Wilhelm Friedrich Hegel, *Lectures on the Philosophy of Religion*, vol. 2, London: Kegan Paul, 1895, pp. 50f.

3 Ibid., p. 51.

4 Ibid., p. 52.

5 Ibid., p. 49.

6 Ibid.

7 Ibid., p. 52 (transl. mod.)

8 Ibid., p. 48.

9 Ibid., p. 52.

10 *The Blue Cliff Record*, p. 77.

11 Eihei Dōgen, *Shobogenzo-zuimonki*, Tokyo: Sotoshu Shumucho, 2015, p. 144.

12 Hegel, *Lectures on the Philosophy of Religion*, vol. 2, p. 48 (transl. amended).

13 Ibid., p. 51.

14 Ibid., p. 49.

15 Ibid., p. 50.

16 Ibid., p. 48.

17 Ibid., p. 56.

18 Ibid., p. 62.

19 Ibid., p. 59. Transl. note: *An-sich-selbst-Saugen* literally means 'sucking oneself'. The context is the 'image of Buddha': 'The image of Buddha is in this thinking position: the feet and arms are folded over one another so that one toe goes into the mouth, representing this returning into self, this self-absorption' (ibid.).

20 Ibid., p. 57 (transl. mod.).

21 Ibid., p. 60.

22 Ibid., p. 61.

23 Ibid., p. 62 (transl. mod.).

24 Ibid., pp. 55f. (transl. mod.)

25 Ibid., p. 19.

26 Ibid., p. 91. Transl. note: the translation of *ausschließende Subjektivität* as 'exclusive subjectivity' has been retained; however, it should be kept in mind that *ausschließend* also carries the active meaning of 'excluding'.

27 Lin-chi, *The Zen Teachings of Master Lin-Chi: A Translation of the Lin-Chi Lu*, trans. Burton Watson, Boston and London: Shambhala, 1993, p. 52.

28 Hegel, *Lectures on the Philosophy of Religion*, vol. 2, p. 57 and p. 56.

29 Ibid., p. 53 (transl. amended).

30 Georg Wilhelm Friedrich Hegel, *Lectures on the Philosophy of Religion*, vol. 3, London: Kegan Paul, 1895, p. 112.

31 *The Blue Cliff Record*, p. 76.

32 *The Ox and His Herdsman: A Chinese Zen Text with Commentary and Pointers by Master D. R. Otsu and Japanese illustrations of the fifteenth century*, trans. M. H. Trevor, Tokyo: Hokuseido Press, 1969, p. 80.

33 Eihei Dōgen, *Shōbōgenzō / The True Darma-Eye Treasury*, 4 vols., trans. Gudo Wafu Nishijima and Chodo Cross; here vol. II., Berkeley: Numata Center for Buddhist Translation and Research, 2008, p. 270 (note 22). This edition explains the important concepts of the *Shōbōgenzō*, which are given not only in transliteration but also in Japanese or Chinese. In addition, there is a glossary of Sanskrit terms at the end of each volume.

34 François Jullien's subtle interpretation of Chinese thought

is centred on the concept of immanence. See his *Detour and Access: Strategies of Meaning in China and Greece*, New York: Zone Books, 2000.

35 Master Yunmen, *From the Record of the Chan Master 'Gate of the Clouds'*, New York: Kodansha, 1994, p. 195.

36 Eihei Dōgen, *Shōbōgenzō / The True Darma-Eye Treasury*, vol. I, Moraga: BDK America Inc., 2007, p. 135. Transl. note: Han's German text has 'Wir müssen das ganze Universum in einem einzigen Staubkörnchen erblicken', which literally translates as 'We need to see the whole universe in a speck of dust.'

37 *The Ox and His Herdsman*, p. 80.

38 Ibid., p. 20.

39 Ibid., p. 80.

40 Master Yunmen, *'Gate of the Clouds'*, p. 97 (note 1).

41 Gottfried Wilhelm Leibniz, 'Principles of Nature and Grace, Based on Reason', in *Philosophical Essays*, Cambridge: Cambridge University Press, 1989, pp. 206–13; here: p. 210.

42 Gottfried Wilhelm Leibniz, 'The Principles of Philosophy, or, the Monadology', in *Philosophical Essays*, pp. 213–25; here: p. 218.

43 *The Ox and His Herdsman*, p. 22.

44 Ibid., p. 86.

45 Martin Heidegger, *The Principle of Reason*, Bloomington: Indiana University Press, 1991, p. 35.

46 Ibid. p. 68.

47 See François Jullien, *In Praise of Blandness: Proceeding from Chinese Thought and* Aesthetics, New York: Zone Books, 2004.

48 Martin Heidegger, 'Why Poets?', in *Off the Beaten Track*, Cambridge: Cambridge University Press, 2002, pp. 200–41; here: p. 200.

49 Martin Heidegger, *Identity and Difference*, New York: Harper and Row, p. 72.

50 Martin Heidegger, '. . . Poetically Man Dwells . . .', in *Poetry, Language, Thought*, New York: HarperCollins, 1975, pp. 209–27; here: pp. 223.

51 Ibid., p. 221.

52 See Byung-Chul Han, *Martin Heidegger: Eine Einführung*, Munich, 1999, pp. 119–39.

53 See ibid., pp. 140–75. – The literal meaning of the German word for 'vermin', *Ungeziefer*, is, etymologically, 'animal that is unsuitable to be sacrificed to God'.

54 Robert Hass (ed.), *The Essential Haiku: Versions of Bashō, Buson, and Issa*, trans. Robert Hass, Hopewell: The Ecco Press, 1994, p. 167.

55 Ibid., p. 39.

56 Arthur Schopenhauer, *The World as Will and Representation*, vol. 2, New York: Dover, 1966, p. 614.

57 Meister Eckhart, *The Complete Mystical Works of Meister Eckhart*, New York: Herder & Herder, 2009, p. 292.

58 Ibid., p. 293.

59 Ibid., p. 422 (transl. amended).

60 Exodus 3:14.

61 Meister Eckhart, *Expositio Libri Exodi*, n. 16, quoted after: *Deutsche Predigten und Traktate*, Munich: Hanser, 1963, pp. 34f.; my translation, drawing on 'Commentary on Exodus', trans. Bernhard McGinn, in *Meister Eckhart: Teacher and Preacher*, Mahwah: The Paulist Press, 1986, pp. 41–145; here: p. 46.

62 Meister Eckhart, *Deutsche Predigten und Traktate*, pp. 34f.

63 Rudolf Otto, *Mysticism East and West*, London: Macmillan, 1932, p. 169.

64 Eckhart, *Complete Mystical Works*, p. 292. Transl. note: 'making' translates *Machen-schaften*. The hyphenation stresses the aspect of making as an activity. As a compound noun, however, *Machenschaften* means 'machinations', and hence carries a negative connotation.

65 Ibid., p. 294.

66 Ibid., p. 318.

67 Ibid., pp. 318f.

68 Ibid., p. 465 (transl. amended).

69 Ibid., p. 317.

70 Ibid., p. 110.

71 Ibid., p. 338.

72 Ibid., p. 296.

73 Ibid., p. 514. Transl. note: *Gelassenheit* [*gelâzenheit*] is an important notion in Eckhart, though he uses the noun only once: 'A question: "Should one willingly forgo all God's sweetness? May this not easily stem from laziness or insufficient love of God?" Certainly, if one does not understand the difference. For we can tell whether it comes from laziness or from true detachment and *self-abandonment* by observing whether, when we feel in this state, when we feel inwardly *completely detached*, we are just as much devoted to God as if we felt Him most strongly; if we do in this state just what we should do – no more and no less – keeping free and detached from all comfort and help, as we should do when we were aware of God's presence' (p. 514; emphasis added). *Gelassenheit* is here translated as 'self-abandonment', while 'completely detached' translates *ganz gelassen*. In fact, *lassen* and *gelassen* are the terms that mainly express the notion in question. They are translated in various ways in the English edition, in the quotation of the main text, for instance, as 'leave-taking' and 'takes leave'. The German, however, puts the emphasis not on an active 'taking' but rather on a passive 'letting go'. Thus, the German sentence 'Das Höchste und Äußerste, was der Mensch lassen kann, das ist, daß er Gott um Gottes willen lasse' could also be translated as 'The highest and ultimate a human can let go of is when he lets go of God for the sake of God.'

74 Ibid., p. 110.

75 Ibid., p. 424.

76 Ibid., p. 429.

77 Transl. note: the German *Zu-Grunde-Gehen* means 'to perish' but here implies 'getting to the bottom of things'.

78 Ibid., pp. 422f.

79 Ibid., p. 421.

80 Ibid., p. 264. Transl. note: Eckhart's *mitewesen* has been rendered into modern German as *Beisein* (literally: being alongside), not as accident. The English translation uses 'admixture' for *Beisein*.

81 Matsuo Bashō, *Bashō's Haiku: Selected Poems of Matsuo Bashō*, New York: SUNY Press, 2004, p. 98.

82 *The Ox and His Herdsman*, p. 21.

83 Ibid., p. 23.

84 Ibid., p. 59.

85 Friedrich Nietzsche, *Thus Spoke Zarathustra*, Cambridge: Cambridge University Press, 2006, p. 244.

86 Ibid., p. 228.

87 Ibid., p. 240.

88 Bashō, *Bashō's Haiku*, p. 56.

89 Lin-chi, *The Zen Teachings of Master Lin-Chi*, p. 77.

90 Eihei Dōgen, *Shōbōgenzō / The True Dharma-Eye Treasury*, vol. III, Moraga: BDK America Inc., 2008, p. 296.

91 Master Yunmen, *'Gate of the Clouds'*, p. 100.

92 Dōgen, *Shōbōgenzō / The True Dharma-Eye Treasury*, vol. III, p. 293.

93 Master Yunmen, *'Gate of the Clouds'*, p. 161.

94 *The Blue Cliff Record*, p. 329.

95 See Master Yunmen, *'Gate of the Clouds'*, p. 224:

> Yunmen asked Caoshan, 'What is the practice of a monk?'
> Caoshan replied, 'Eating rice from the monastery fields.'
> Yunmen said, 'And if one does just that?'
> Caoshan replied, 'Can you really eat it?'
> Yunmen said, 'Yes, I can.'
> Caoshan: 'How do you do that?'
> Yunmen: 'What is difficult about putting on clothes and eating rice?'
> Caoshan said, 'Why don't you say that you're wearing a hide and have horns [like an animal]?'
> Yunmen bowed.

96 See Eugen Herrigel, *Der Zen-Weg*, Weilheim: Otto Wilhelm Barth Verlag, 1970, p. 40.

97 Ibid., p. 39.

98 Master Yunmen, *'Gate of the Clouds'*, p. 167.

99 Ibid., p. 212.

100 Martin Heidegger, *Being and Time*, Oxford: Blackwell, 1962, p. 423.

101 Ibid., p. 422.

102 Ibid., p. 396.
103 Ibid.
104 Ibid., p. 322.
105 Ibid., p. 314.
106 *The Ox and His Herdsman*, p. 86.
107 Martin Heidegger, *The Fundamental Concepts of Metaphysics: World, Finitude, Solitude*, Bloomington: Indiana University Press, 1995, pp. 148f.
108 Master Yunmen, '*Gate of the Clouds*', p. 93.
109 *The Ox and His Herdsman*, p. 5.
110 Ibid., p. 40 (transl. mod.). Transl. note: the English edition has 'wherever we talk or stand', the German 'Denn wo wir auch gehen und stehen', i.e. 'wherever we walk or stand', so I have corrected the translation.
111 Mumon Ekai, *Mumonkan: The Zen Masterpiece*, trans. R. H. Blyth, Tokyo: The Hokuseido Press, 2002 [1966], p. 147.
112 Master Yunmen, '*Gate of the Clouds*', p. 209.
113 *The Blue Cliff Record*, p. 40.
114 Mumon Ekai, *Mumonkan*, p. 153.

Emptiness

1 Bashō, *Bashō's Haiku*, p. 47.
2 Ibid., p. 123.
3 Dōgen, *Shōbōgenzō / The True Dharma-Eye Treasury*, vol. I, p. 218.
4 Ibid., p. 221.
5 Ibid.
6 See ibid., pp. 221f.
7 *The Ox and His Herdsman*, p. 60. Transl. note: the German edition is inspired by Heidegger and translates the last sentence as 'Das eine Wesen west an in allem Anwesenden und alles Anwesende scheint in das eine Wesen' ('The one being presences in all that is presencing and all presencing shines into the one being'). See *Der Ochs und sein Hirte*, Eine altchinesische Zen-Geschichte erläutert von Meister Daizohkutsu R. Ohtsu, mit japanischen Bildern aus dem 15. Jahrhundert, Pfullingen: Neske, 1981 [1958], p. 94.

8 Dōgen, Shōbōgenzō / *The True Dharma-Eye Treasury*, vol. I, p. 223.

9 Ibid., p. 225 (transl. amended). Transl. note: the English edition has 'We should remember the fact that mountains like sages and the fact that [mountains] like saints.' I have brought the passage in line with the German version.

10 *The Ox and His Herdsman*, p. 92.

11 Dōgen, *Shōbōgenzō* / *The True Dharma-Eye Treasury*, vol. III, p. 230.

12 *The Blue Cliff Record*, p. 82. Transl. note: the English edition corresponds closely to Han's introduction of the quotation: 'When snow covers the white flowers, it's hard to distinguish the outlines.' I have given a translation of the German version.

13 Ibid., p. 214.

14 Transl. note: the German version gives *Einfarbigkeit* ('monochromaticity') where the English has 'uniformity'.

15 Master Yunmen, *'Gate of the Clouds'*, p. 160.

16 Dōgen, *Shōbōgenzō* / *The True Dharma-Eye Treasury*, vol. I, p. 43.

17 Transl. note: as a footnote in the *Mumonkan* explains, a tenzo is '[o]ne of the six classes of monks in office' (p. 262).

18 Ekai, *Mumonkan*, pp. 262f.

19 Martin Héidegger, 'The Thing', in *Poetry, Language, Thought*, New York: HarperCollins, 1975, pp. 161–84; here: pp. 169f.

20 Ibid., p. 170. Transl. note: in the German, the last sentence is 'Im Wesen des Kruges weilen Erde und Himmel.' A more literal translation would be 'Earth and sky rest in the essence of the jug.' Note that Heidegger also uses the term *Wesen* as a nominalized verb. Thus, the sentence could be translated 'Earth and sky dwell in the essencing of the jug.' The notion of 'essence'/'essencing', rather than 'jugness', is needed for the argument that follows.

21 Ibid., pp. 170f.

22 Bashō, *Bashō's Haiku*, p. 32.

23 Ibid., p. 177.

24 Ibid. Transl. note: in the existing English translation, Heidegger's *Einfalt* is variably rendered as 'onefold', 'simplicity' or 'simpleness'. It should be kept in mind that the German

term is always *Einfalt*, setting up an opposition to *Geviert*, or 'fourfold'.

25 Ibid.
26 Ibid.
27 Ibid., pp. 177f.
28 Ibid., p. 178.
29 Heidegger, '. . . Poetically Man Dwells . . .', p. 220.
30 Martin Heidegger, 'A Dialogue on Language (between a Japanese and an Inquirer)', in *On the Way to Language*, New York: Harper & Row, 1971, pp. 1–54; here: p. 18.
31 Transl. note: more literally, 'the hollow centre' [*hohle Mitte*].
32 Martin Heidegger, *Contributions to Philosophy (Of the Event)*, Bloomington: Indiana University Press, 2012, p. 268.
33 Martin Heidegger, 'Art and Space', in Neil Leach (ed.), *Rethinking Architecture: A Reader in Cultural Theory*, London: Routledge, 1997, pp. 116–19; here: pp. 118f. (transl. amended).
34 Martin Heidegger, 'Language in the Poem: A Discussion on Georg Trakl's Poetic Work', in *On the Way to Language*, pp. 159–98; here: pp. 159f.
35 Bashō, *Bashō's Haiku*, p. 143 (transl. mod.).

No one

1 Bashō, *Bashō's Haiku*, p. 153.
2 Transl. note: *conatus* is usually translated as 'effort', 'endeavour' or 'striving'. However, I here follow Han, who uses *Wille*.
3 Leibniz, 'Principles of Nature and Grace, Based on Reason', p. 207.
4 Martin Heidegger, *Nietzsche*, vol. 2, Pfullingen: Neske, 1961, p. 449.
5 Leibniz, 'Principles of Nature and Grace, Based on Reason', p. 210.
6 Heidegger, *Nietzsche*, vol. 2, p. 449.
7 Leibniz, 'The Principles of Philosophy, or, the Monadology', p. 219.
8 *The Ox and His Herdsman*, p. 33.
9 *Bi-yän-lu: Meister Yüan-wu's Niederschrift von der Smaragdenen Felswand*, 3 vols., trans. and ed. by Wilhelm Gundert, Munich: Hanser, 1960–1973; here vol. 1, p. 145. Transl. note: the quo-

tation is part of the editor's commentary and hence not in the English edition.

10 Hui Hai, 'Hui Hai on Sudden Illumination', in *The Zen Teaching of Hui Hai on Sudden Illumination*, London: Rider, 1962, pp. 43–85; here: p. 46.

11 Johann Gottlieb Fichte, *The Vocation of Man*, Chicago: The Open Court Publishing Company, 1931, p. 32.

12 Georg Wilhelm Friedrich Hegel, *Naturphilosophie*, vol. 1: *Die Vorlesung von 1819/20*, Naples: Bibliopolis, 1982, p. 66.

13 Georg Wilhelm Friedrich Hegel, *Hegel's Philosophy of Nature: Part II of the Encyclopaedia of the Philosophical Sciences (1830)*, Oxford: Oxford University Press, 1970, § 351, p. 353.

14 Ibid., § 303, p. 149.

15 Bashō, *Bashō's Haiku*, p. 112.

16 Keiji Nishitani, 'The Japanese Art of Arranged Flowers', in Robert C. Solomon and Kathleen M. Higgins (eds.), *World Philosophy: A Text with Readings*, New York: McGraw Hill, 1995, pp. 23–7; here: p. 26.

17 Transl. note: 'document' translates *Zeugnis* and 'illustration' translates *Beleg*. Both German terms imply positive evidence: *Zeugnis* may mean testimony, evidence; *Beleg* may even mean 'proof'.

18 Heidegger, *Being and Time*, p. 242. Transl. note: the fable of Cura is no. 220 of the fables of Hyginus.

19 Ibid., p. 243.

20 Transl. note: the German expression 'um meiner selbst willen' contains the idea that I have the 'will' to do something in my own interest.

21 Ibid., p. 225.

22 Ibid., p. 314.

23 Martin Heidegger, *The Basic Problems of Phenomenology*, Bloomington: Indiana University Press, 1982, pp. 276f.

24 Heidegger, *Being and Time*, p. 373.

25 Ibid., p. 378.

26 See Keiji Nishitani, *Religion and Nothingness*, Berkeley: University of California Press, 1982, p. 164.

27 Hass (ed.), *The Essential Haiku*, p. 170. Transl. note: the

German version of this haiku translates as: Though not a Buddha / So oblivious of self / Stands the old pine tree

28 Johann Wolfgang Goethe, *Faust: Part I*, London: Penguin, 2005, ll. 1110–13:

> You only know the one impulse. Oh may
> The other never come into your ken.
> Alas, I house two souls in me
> And each from each wants separation.

29 Quoted from Kooichi Tsujimura, 'Über Yü-Chiens Landschaftsbild *In die ferne Bucht kommen Segelboote zurück*', in *Die Philosophie der Kyôto-Schule: Texte und Einführung*, ed. and introduced by Ryōsuke Ōhashi, Freiburg: Alber, 2011, pp. 426–39; here: p. 428.

30 Ibid., p. 433.

31 Ibid., p. 431.

32 Transl. note: originally, Noh actors were exclusively male. Things changed in the course of the twentieth century, and there are now roughly 1,200 professional male and 200 professional female actors. I have used the male form in the following, in line with the German original, and also because the reflexive forms would have made other solutions extremely cumbersome.

33 Zhuangzi, *The Complete Works of Zhuangzi*, New York: Columbia University Press, 2013, p. 18.

34 Apart from the sliding movements, there is a stomping with one leg (*fumu*).

35 Martin Heidegger, 'Summary of a Lecture on "Time and Being"', in *On Time and Being*, New York: Harper & Row, 1972, pp. 25–54; here: p. 39.

36 Ibid., pp. 39f.

37 Ibid., p. 38. Transl. note: 'there is' translates *es gibt*, which literally translates as 'it gives', a fact invoked by Heidegger.

38 Bashō, *Bashō's Haiku*, p. 91.

39 Hass (ed.), *The Essential Haiku*, p. 125.

Dwelling nowhere

1 Hass (ed.), *The Essential Haiku*, p. 54.
2 Matsuo Bashō, *Oku No Hosomichi – The Narrow Road to the Deep North*, trans. and ed. by Tim Chilcott, available at the editor's website: http://www.tclt.org.uk/basho/Oku_2011.pdf, p. 3.
3 Transl. note: This passage is not part of the English edition. Translated from the German version in Matsuo Bashō, *Auf schmalen Pfaden durchs Hinterland*, Mainz: Dieterich'sche Verlagsbuchhandlung, 2011, p. 42.
4 Ibid., pp. 96ff. In the culture of the Far East, which probably leans more towards impermanence and transformation than identity and permanence, the word 'wind' is used very frequently. 'Landscape', for instance, means 'view of wind'. Instead of a 'landscape' one actually should talk of a 'windscape'. From this Far Eastern perspective, 'landscape' loses the sense of something rigid attached to the earth and acquires the sense of something flowing or passing.
5 Bashō, *Oku No Hosomichi*, p. 47.
6 Keiji Nishitani, 'Die 'Verrücktheit' beim Dichter Bashō', in *Die Philosophie der Kyôto-Schule*, pp. 258–80; here: p. 278.
7 Bashō, *Bashō's Haiku*, p. 38.
8 Transl. note: the German *Gemach* means both 'slowness' and 'chamber' or 'room'.
9 Bashō, *Bashō's Haiku*, p. 88.
10 Ibid., p. 116.
11 See Martin Lehnert, *Die Strategie eines Kommentars zum Diamant-Sûtra*, Wiesbaden: Harrassowitz, 1999, p. 132.
12 Dōgen, *Shobogenzo-zuimonki*, pp. 194f.
13 Transl. note: the preceding passage is built on forms of *lassen* (letting go): *sich lassen, von sich ablassen, sich vergehen lassen, Gelassenheit*. See also the discussion of Eckhart's *Gelassenheit* above (ch. 1, note. 73).
14 See Dōgen, *Shōbōgenzō / The True Dharma-Eye Treasury*, vol. II, p. 151.
15 Emmanuel Levinas, 'The Trace of the Other', in Mark C. Taylor (ed.), *Deconstruction in Context: Literature and Philosophy*, Chicago: Chicago University Press, 1986, pp. 345–59; here: p. 346.

16 Ibid., p. 348.
17 Genesis 12: 4–5.
18 Genesis 12: 1–3.
19 Genesis 13: 14–18.
20 Genesis 15: 7–8.
21 Søren Kierkegaard, *Fear and Trembling*, Princeton: Princeton University Press, 1983, p. 115.
22 Bashō, *Bashō's Haiku*, p. 74.
23 Lin-Chi, *The Zen Teachings of Master Lin-Chi*, p. 55.
24 Transl. note: in German, *Indifferenz* and *Gleichgültigkeit* both mean 'indifference'. However, the compound noun *Gleichgültigkeit* consists of *gleich* ('same') and *Gültigkeit* ('validity'), thus conveying the idea that everything has equal validity, whereas 'Indifferenz' emphasizes uninterestedness.
25 Plato, 'Apology' (40c), in *Complete Works*, Indianapolis: Hackett, 1997, pp. 17–36; here: p. 35.
26 Plato, 'Phaedo' (80e), in *Complete Works*, pp. 49–100; here: p. 71 (emph. B.-Ch. H.).
27 Ibid., 84b, p. 73.
28 Ibid., 83e, p. 73.
29 Plato, 'Phaedrus' (246c), in *Complete Works*, pp. 506–56; here: p. 524 (transl. mod.). Transl. note: the German text has *unterwegs sein* (literally 'being on the way') as the quotation from Plato. However, the English translation has: 'All soul looks after all that lacks a soul, and patrols all of heaven, taking different shapes at different times.' Hence the singular form needed to be changed to plural.
30 Ibid. (247e; transl. mod.). Transl. note: see previous endnote; the singular form had to be changed to plural again.
31 Plato, 'Republic' (398a), in *Complete Works*, pp. 971–1223; here: p. 1035. Transl. note: the German version has *freundlich* – 'friendly', a key term in Han's text – where the English has 'pleasing'.
32 Ibid. (397e–398a). Transl. note: the English and German versions differ. A more literal translation of the German would be: 'who because of his wisdom can appear in many forms and represent all things'.
33 Ibid. (388e), p. 1026.

34 See Plato, 'Phaedrus' (246a-e), pp. 524f.
35 Plato, 'Phaedo' (81a), p, 71.
36 *The Ox and his Herdsman*, p. 83.
37 Ibid., p. 86.
38 Ibid., p. 82.

Death

1 Martin Heidegger, *Hegel*, Bloomington: Indiana University Press, 2015, p. 19.
2 Robert N. Huey, 'Journal of My Father's Last Days. Issa's Chichi no Shūen Nikki', *Monumenta Nipponica*, vol. 39, no. 1 (1984), pp. 25–54; here: p. 49. Transl. note: The English and German versions differ. Transl. amended to bring it in line with the German text.
3 Plato, *Phaedo* (81a, 80b), p. 71 and p. 70.
4 Ibid. (64a), p. 55.
5 Ibid. (80e), p. 71.
6 Ibid. (66e–67b), p. 58.
7 Ibid. (80d), p. 71.
8 Bashō, *Bashō's Haiku*, p. 43.
9 Hegel, *Hegel's Philosophy of Nature*, § 375, p. 441.
10 Georg Wilhelm Friedrich Hegel, *Hegel's Aesthetics: Lectures on Fine Arts*, vol. I, Oxford: Clarendon, 1975, pp. 537f.
11 Transl. note: 'Er *richtet* das Endliche zu *Grunde*.' *Richten* by itself can mean 'to judge' or 'to set in order', 'repair'. *Zu Grunde richten*, however, literally means 'to wreck', 'to ruin'. But within the context of the passage, *Grund* also takes on the meaning of 'foundation' (of the general). And finally, *Grund* can also mean the 'reason' for something, another relevant semantic dimension in the passage.
12 Hegel, *Lectures on the Philosophy of Religion*, vol. 1, pp. 181f.
13 Georg Wilhelm Friedrich Hegel, *The Phenomenology of Spirit*, Cambridge: Cambridge University Press, 2018, pp. 20f. (emphasis added, B.-Ch. H.).
14 Fichte, *The Vocation of Man*, p. 174.
15 Ibid., p. 175 (transl. amended).
16 Ibid.
17 Ibid., p. 174.

18 Ibid., pp. 175f.
19 Matsuo Bashō, *The Essential Bashō*, trans. Sam Hamill, Boston: Shambhala, 1999, p. 98.
20 Heidegger, *Being and Time*, p. 307.
21 Ibid., p. 308.
22 Ibid., p. 233. Transl. note: the English edition has 'Everyday familiarity collapses', a perfectly accurate but rather terse rendering of the more dramatic German 'Die alltägliche Vertrautheit bricht in sich zusammen' – 'Everyday familiarity collapses in on itself'. As *Vertrautheit* not only means 'familiar' but also implies *vertrauen* ('to trust'), the sentence expresses not just the disappearance of something familiar but also the collapse of trust in the world.
23 Ibid., p. 234.
24 Ibid., p. 394.
25 Ibid., p. 344.
26 Ibid., p. 307.
27 See Byung-Chul Han, *Todesarten: Philosophische Untersuchungen zum Tod*, Munich: Wilhelm Fink, 1998, pp. 38–73. Transl. note: 're-*minded*' translates *er-innert*, suggesting an inward-pointing process.
28 Martin Heidegger, *History of the Concept of Time: Prolegomena*, Bloomington: Indiana University Press, 1985, p. 313.
29 Heidegger, *Being and Time*, p. 308 and p. 344.
30 Bashō, *Bashō's Haiku*, p. 103. Transl. note: a more literal translation of the German version would be: 'Poor worm in the rape / butterfly you'll never be / and perish in autumn.'
31 Fichte, *The Vocation of Man*, p. 176.
32 Quoted after Dumoulin, *A History of Zen Buddhism*, p. 152.
33 Quoted after ibid., p. 159.
34 Issa, *Die letzten Tage meines Vaters*, Mainz: Dieterich, 1985, p. 123. Transl. note: this passage is not part of the English translation.
35 Dōgen, *Shobogenzo-zuimonki*, p. 27.
36 Ibid., p. 113.
37 Heidegger, *Being and Time*, p. 311.
38 *The Blue Cliff Record*, p. 208.
39 Meister Eckhart, *Selected Writings*, London: Penguin, 1994,

p. 248. Transl. note: this sermon is not included in the *Complete Mystical Works*.

40 Eckhart, *The Complete Mystical Works*, p. 404.
41 Eckhart, *Selected Writings*, p. 248.
42 Eckhart, *The Complete Mystical Works*, p. 405.
43 Ibid., p. 404.
44 Ibid., p. 403.
45 Ibid., p. 404.
46 Eckhart, *Selected Writings*, pp. 247f.
47 *The Blue Cliff Record*, p. 215. Transl. note: in the German edition quoted by Han, the last sentence is worded more strongly: 'It is the place where when it is cold, the cold kills you, and where when it is warm, the heat kills you.'
48 Ibid., p. 217.
49 Ibid., pp. 262f. Transl. note: there are various differences between the German and English versions. In particular the last sentence of the German has a definite rather than indefinite article, and translates as: 'At these words Jianyuan, at a stroke, saw the light', or 'was illuminated'.
50 Ibid., p. 262. Transl. note: the German version speaks of a 'still verborgene ganze Wahrheit', a 'secretly hidden full truth'.
51 Dōgen, *Shōbōgenzō / The True Dharma-Eye Treasury*, vol. I, p. 42.
52 *The Blue Cliff Record*, p. 210. Transl. note: a more literal translation of the German version would be: 'Only once the dead in you has been fully killed will you see yourself as someone living; and only once the one alive in you has become fully alive will you see yourself as someone dead.'

Friendliness

1 Transl. note: My translation from the German version. The English version differs significantly from the German and does not bring out the point of the argument: 'Yangshan asked Sansheng, "What's your name?" ... Sansheng said, "Hug." ... Yangshan said, "Hug? That's me." ... Sansheng said, "My name is Huiran." ... Yangshan laughed.' *The Blue Cliff Record*, p. 310.

117

2 Transl. note: the English edition parenthetically comments on the question 'What's your name?': 'Name and reality take each other away. He brings in a thief, who will ransack his house.'

3 Ibid., pp. 312f.

4 See *Zen-Worte im Tee-Raume*, with commentary by Sôtei Akaji, Tokyo: Deutsche Gesellschaft für Natur- und Völkerkunde Ostasiens, 1943, p. 21.

5 Georg Wilhelm Friedrich Hegel, 'First Philosophy of Spirit', in *System of Ethical Life (1802/3) and First Philosophy of Spirit (Part III of the System of Speculative Philosophy 1803/4)*, Albany: SUNY, 1979, pp. 187–250; here: p. 236.

6 Ibid. p. 238.

7 Ibid., p. 240.

8 Ibid.

9 *The Ox and His Herdsman*, p. 24.

10 Ibid., p. 92.

11 Friedrich Nietzsche, *Daybreak*, Cambridge: Cambridge University Press, 1997, p. 470.

12 *The Ox and His Herdsman*, p. 88.

13 Hass (ed.) *The Essential Haiku*, p. 54.

14 Aristotle, *Nicomachean Ethics*, Oxford: Oxford University Press, 2009, 1166a, ll. 29–32; p. 169.

15 Ibid., 1166b, l. 1.

16 Aristotle, *The Eudemian Ethics of Aristotle*, New Brunswick: Transaction, 2013, 1245a, ll. 35–9, p. 170 (transl. amended).

17 Montaigne, 'On Friendship', in *Essays*, London: Penguin, 1993, Book 1, Chapter 28, pp. 91–105; here: p. 103. Transl. note: Montaigne's text is interspersed with quotations from classical authors, in both Latin and in translation, that are set off from his prose. One such insertion is left out in the German; one is integrated into the running text. I follow the German original in not indicating the omission, but I set off the quotation that is integrated in the German text.

18 Aristotle, *The Eudemian Ethics*, 1236a, ll. 14–15, p. 141.

19 See Aristotle, *Nicomachean Ethics*, 1155b, ll. 27ff., p. 143f.

20 Aristotle, *The Eudemian Ethics*, 1242a, ll. 9–11, p. 161.

21 Aristotle, *Nicomachean Ethics*, 1161b, l. 29, p. 157.

22 Ibid., 1169b, ll. 12–13, p. 176.
23 Dōgen, *Shobogenzo-zuimonki*, p. 113.
24 Luke 6: 34–35 and 38.
25 Herrigel, *Der Zen-Weg*, p. 91.
26 'Die Dialoge des Huang Po mit seinen Schülern', in *Meditations-Sutras des Mahânâ-Buddhismus*, ed. by Raoul von Muralt, vol. 2, Berne: Origo, 1988, p. 77.
27 On the term 'Gleich-Gültigkeit' see above, ch. 4, note 24.
28 Arthur Schopenhauer, *The World as Will and Representation*, vol. 1, New York: Dover, 1969, p. 372.
29 Ibid.
30 Arthur Schopenhauer, *The Basis of Morality*, London: Swan, Sonnenschein & Co., 1903, p. 169.
31 Ibid., p. 277. Transl. note: here, and in the following quotations from *The Basis of Morality*, emphasis in the German original that is absent in the English translation has been reinstated.
32 Schopenhauer, *The World as Will and Representation*, vol. 1, p. 373. Transl. note: the German is even more forceful: 'sich, sein Selbst, seinen Willen', that is, 'himself, his self, his will'.
33 Schopenhauer, *The Basis of Morality*, pp. 169f.
34 Ibid., p. 170.
35 Ibid., p. 174.
36 Martin Buber, 'What is Man?', in *Between Man and Man*, London: Routledge, 2002, pp. 140–244; here: p. 243.
37 Ibid., pp. 241f. (emph. B.-Ch. H.) Transl. note: a more literal translation would be 'no longer located, as usual, either in the inwardness of the individuals or in a general world that comprehends and determines them, but in fact *between* them'.
38 Ibid., p. 244.
39 Ibid., p. 242.
40 Martin Buber, *I and Thou*, Edinburgh: T. and T. Clarke, 1937, p. 8.
41 Ibid., p. 78.
42 Ibid., p. 16.
43 Ibid., p. 17.
44 Ibid., pp. 5f.
45 Ibid., p. 75.

46 Ibid.
47 Ibid., p. 101.
48 Ibid., p. 75.
49 Ibid., p. 100.
50 Martin Buber, 'Dialogue', in *Between Man and Man*, pp. 1–45; here: p. 18.
51 Buber, *I and Thou*, p. 115.
52 See ibid., pp. 15f.
53 See ibid., pp. 8f. Transl. note: '*determines*' translates '*Be-stimmung*', a neologism that expresses the double meaning of 'determining' and 'bestowing a mood' (*Stimmung*) on something.
54 Ibid., p. 92
55 Ibid.
56 Ibid., p. 93.
57 Bashō, *Bashō's Haiku*, p. 132. Transl. note: a more literal rendering of the German version would be: 'No one to be seen / as if behind a mirror / the plum blossom in spring.'
58 Issa, *Die letzten Tage meines Vaters*, p. 98. Transl. note: this quotation is not part of the English translation.
59 *Ficus glomerata*, a species of fig tree.
60 Dōgen, *Shōbōgenzō / The True Dharma-Eye Treasury*, vol. III, p. 325.
61 Ibid., p. 325.
62 Ibid., p. 327.